INTEGRATION WITHOUT MEMBERSHIP

SWITZERLAND'S BILATERAL AGREEMENTS WITH THE EUROPEAN UNION

MARIUS VAHL

AND

NINA GROLIMUND

CENTRE FOR EUROPEAN POLICY STUDIES

BRUSSELS

This study on relations between Switzerland and the EU has been undertaken by the Centre for European Policy Studies (CEPS) in collaboration with the Europe Institute of the University of Zürich (EIZ). The authors gratefully acknowledge the support of the Office for Economy and Labour of the Canton of Zürich, which allowed this study to be made. Appreciation is also expressed to experts and EU and Swiss officials for comments on an earlier draft of this report, and to George Dura at CEPS for research assistance. The views expressed in this study, including the interpretations of the position of EU and Swiss officials, are those of the authors alone.

Marius Vahl is a Research Fellow at CEPS and a PhD candidate at the Catholic University of Leuven. *Nina Grolimund* is a Research Fellow at the Europe Institute of the University of Zürich.

ISBN 92-9079-616-2

Centre for European Policy Studies
Place du Congrès 1, B-1000 Brussels
Tel: 32 (0) 2 229.39.11 Fax: 32 (0) 2 219.41.51
e-mail: info@ceps.be
internet: http://www.ceps.be

CONTENTS

List of Boxes

EXECUTIVE SUMMARY

A comprehensive sets of bilateral sectoral agreements. Switzerland and the European Union concluded two sets of bilateral sectoral agreements between 1994 and 2004. The first set of agreements – known as Bilateral I – entered into force in June 2002. The second set of agreements – known as Bilateral II – was signed in 2004. As a result of these agreements, Switzerland is more closely integrated with the EU than any non-member state, with the exception of its EFTA partners Norway, Iceland and Liechtenstein. Previously limited mainly to economic affairs, EU-Swiss relations are increasingly moving into other areas such as the field of justice and home affairs.

The bilateral agreements function well. The principal conclusion of this study is that overall, the bilateral sectoral agreements that entered into force in June 2002 – Bilateral I – function well. There have been no significant conflicts or disputes between the EU and Switzerland over the agreements and implementation has proceeded smoothly. This assessment was shared by virtually all of the officials interviewed as part of the study.

Full implementation will occur only in the next decade. Most of the agreements of Bilaterals I and II include significant transition periods, and many agreements of Bilateral II have not yet entered into force. Full implementation of all 16 agreements in the two packages will only occur towards the middle of the next decade. It is therefore too early to fully assess the impact of Bilaterals I and II, and thus of the bilateral sectoral approach as a model of integration without membership.

Minor problems encountered with Bilateral I. In spite of this, a number of (actual and potential) problems and deficiencies related to the functioning of the bilateral agreements have been identified. The most prominent general problems that have been encountered include disagreements on the precise delineation of the scope of specific agreements, the role of the European Court of Justice and ECJ case law, and the scope for Swiss derogations. None of these issues, however, has achieved sufficient prominence to trigger the formal dispute settlement mechanisms provided for by the bilateral agreements, with the exception of a case currently pending before the ECJ concerning the Zürich airport in connection with the air transport agreement.

Divergent analyses of the main problems by Switzerland and the EU. EU and Swiss officials appear to have different interpretations of what constitute the most important challenges posed by the bilateral agreements. The principal Swiss concerns are related to a lack of transparency and information about the implementation of the agreements, and the limited access to 'decision-shaping' accorded by the agreements. On the EU side, the main concerns are the practical difficulties in managing the complex set of sectoral EU-Swiss agreements and scepticism towards Swiss attempts at 'cherry picking' EU policies and norms.

Swiss concerns less prominent in more comprehensive agreements. There are indications that some of the problems encountered in particular on the Swiss side are smaller in the more ambitious 'partial integration' agreements, such as air transport and Schengen, than in the more traditional cooperation agreements. If this turns out to be a trend, it would have interesting implications, as these partial integration agreements go further in terms of integration with the EU than most EU third-country agreements.

Difference between the rhetoric and the reality of the Swiss-EU relationship. There seems to be a notable difference between the way the EU-Swiss relationship is portrayed in official Swiss statements and documents and the way the relationship functions in practice, according to Swiss and EU officials. In the former context, emphasis is placed on the 'static' nature of many of the bilateral agreements, the autonomous implementation of the agreements in Switzerland and the fact that the agreements are based on the notion of 'equivalence of laws'. But the reality faced by those in charge of managing the day-to-day relationship is that EU-Swiss relations follow the general pattern in the EU's relations with small neighbouring countries: the EU is the policy-maker and the associate is the policy-taker. Access to the EU market and to EU programmes and agencies takes place on the EU's terms.

Differences and similarities between the Swiss model and the European Economic Area (EEA). While Switzerland has considerably upgraded its relationship with the EU through Bilaterals I and II, it still falls far short of the relationship established between the EU and the EFTA states of the EEA. Switzerland's access to the EU's internal market is much more limited, perhaps most notably exemplified by the absence of an agreement on services. Although the EEA entails more extensive obligations towards the EU, the EEA states are also granted rights, for instance on 'decision-shaping', that are not accorded to Switzerland. In spite of the considerable conceptual and institutional differences between the EEA and the bilateral sectoral approach, the overall balance of rights and obligations appears quite similar.

Not one, but several Swiss models. While it is possible to speak of the bilateral sectoral approach as the 'Swiss model', it is becoming less unique in the EU's external relations, as other third countries, notably among the EU's neighbours, are cooperating and integrating ever more closely with the EU, frequently through the conclusion of sectoral bilateral agreements. Furthermore, the EU-Swiss agreements differ considerably among themselves. Some agreements take the form of more traditional cooperation agreements, while others – such as the agreements on Schengen and air transport – allow for partial Swiss integration with the EU. The latter cases provide possible models for the EU's fledgling European Neighbourhood Policy (ENP), for instance by giving the European Court of Justice a greater role in the process of providing the ENP partners a 'stake in the single market' (the 'Swiss air transport model') or giving the neighbours a more inclusive role in the decision-shaping and -making processes within the EU (the 'Schengen association model').

A dynamic relationship. One of the supposed benefits of the bilateral sectoral approach was that it was a more 'static' model compared with the more 'dynamic' EEA, thus giving greater autonomy to Swiss authorities to determine the scope and depth of cooperation and integration. But this study shows that the relationship between Switzerland and the EU is highly dynamic. Indeed, no other country has seen such a significant upgrade in its relationship with the EU as has Switzerland. It seems clear that this dynamism will continue over the course of the next decade, as new agreements are concluded and existing agreements are adapted, updated and renewed.

Impact of bilateral agreements and the unilateral Europeanisation of Switzerland. The bilateral sectoral agreements have had a considerable direct impact on Switzerland. Combined with the unilateral and pre-emptive Europeanisation of Switzerland in response to the broader process of European integration and globalisation, these have led to important changes to the political and economic system in Switzerland. The main consequence has been to change the balance of power among the main actors in the complex Swiss political system. The power of the executive branch of the federal government has been strengthened. While the power of the Swiss people through direct democracy remains intact, the linkages (legal and political, explicit and implicit) between the agreements compound the consequences of each individual vote on a specific agreement being adopted or amended. Each vote thus becomes a referendum not just on a specific agreement, but on the bilateral sectoral approach and virtually the entire set of agreements between the EU and Switzerland.

Broad satisfaction with the bilateral sectoral approach. In spite of these factors, there is broad support in Switzerland for the current state of the relationship following the conclusion of Bilaterals I and II. Neither the political elite, the major economic interest groups nor the general public are currently inclined to substitute the bilateral sectoral approach in favour of other theoretical alternatives, such as full EU membership or joining the European Economic Area. The EU is content with the overall state of the relationship and is unlikely to seek any fundamental changes to the bilateral sectoral approach with Switzerland. Officials on both sides agree that it is now time to focus on the implementation of the agreements in full and to allow them to function for some years before any debate on more fundamental alternatives can be considered anew.

Potential stumbling blocks. The dynamism of EU-Swiss relations and the sectoral nature of the relationship combined with the peculiarities of the Swiss political system mean, however, that the long-term prospects of the bilateral sectoral approach between Switzerland and the EU are far from assured. There are likely to be numerous occasions in the coming years that could upset the smooth functioning of the bilateral agreements. Further referenda as well as additional negotiations of new agreements combined with the legal and political linkages between the various agreements create an element of uncertainty not just about the specific agreement in question, but about the continuation of the bilateral sectoral approach as such.

1. Introduction

Switzerland appears as one of the great anomalies of European integration. Located at the heart of Western Europe and surrounded by European Union (EU) member states on all sides, it has chosen not to be a member of the EU. Fiercely proud of their sovereignty and independence, the Swiss people have on repeated occasions said 'no' to proposals for further integration. While a referendum on EU membership, the stated goal of the Swiss government since May 1992, has never taken place as such, the Swiss voters rejected participation in the European Economic Area (EEA) together with its partners in the European Free Trade Association (EFTA) in December 1992.

But a closer look reveals that Switzerland is in fact closely integrated with the European Union. In economic terms, the EU is Switzerland's number one trading partner, accounting for more than 60% of total Swiss exports and almost 80% of its imports. Switzerland is the third most important trading partner of the EU, with the volume of bilateral trade approaching €150 billion annually. There are similar patterns as concerns investments.[1]

In fact, it can be claimed that few European countries have attained the level of integration with their EU neighbours as has Switzerland, even among the EU member states themselves. Some 20% of the residents of Switzerland are foreigners, the large majority of whom – more than 850,000 people – are EU citizens, and hundreds of thousands people regularly commute across the Swiss-EU border. This is a higher share of non-EU citizens than found in any EU member state except Luxembourg. EU citizens are even more numerous in certain sectors of the economy,

---

[1] See the Statistical Annex for details.

constituting for instance more than a third of the teaching staff in Swiss universities.

Furthermore, although Switzerland is not a member of the EU, it has an extensive set of bilateral agreements with the Union. Indeed, the EU has concluded more bilateral agreements with Switzerland than with any other third country. Following the 'no' vote to the EEA in late 1992, Switzerland has taken further steps to move closer to the EU. Between 1994 and 2004, the Swiss government negotiated two sets of bilateral sectoral agreements with the EU. The first set of seven such agreements – known as Bilateral I – were concluded in 1998 and entered into force in June 2002. A second set of nine agreements – known as Bilateral II – were signed in October 2004. Negotiations on further agreements are envisaged.

Indeed, the acceleration of the European integration process from the mid-1980s, with the creation of the internal market, economic and monetary union, an 'area of freedom, security and justice', and common foreign, security and defence policies, has arguably had a greater impact on how Switzerland is governed than in many EU member states. These changes have taken place directly as a result of the bilateral agreements, as well as through changes to the Swiss political and constitutional system undertaken primarily to handle Switzerland's relationship with the European Union.

In spite of these developments, EU-Swiss relations have received relatively little attention in the field of European studies. A review of the major social science journals specialised in European integration and searches in research and internet databases reveal a limited number of studies on the subject. Part of the reason for this is perhaps linguistic. The lingua franca of European studies is English. Most of the research conducted on EU-Swiss relations is undertaken by Swiss scholars writing mainly in German or French.

The lack of attention to EU-Swiss relations in the academic literature has a parallel in the European policy debate. There has been a growing interest in EU policy towards its neighbours in recent years. This is a reflection of the considerable developments in the EU's relations with non-members in the wider European area, notably with the creation of the European Neighbourhood Policy (ENP) from 2002 onwards. Whereas this has been accompanied by a considerable interest in the EU's relations with Switzerland's partners in EFTA and the European Economic Area as possible models for EU neighbourhood policy, there has so far not been a corresponding interest in EU-Swiss relations. More than a decade in gestation, Bilaterals I and II are now being implemented in the midst of a serious crisis in the EU, in part due to 'enlargement fatigue'. Whether or not the 'Swiss model' can be made to function can provide important lessons for the EU and the search for a viable model of 'integration without membership'.

This study aims to analyse the functioning of the bilateral agreements between Switzerland and the EU, focusing on the agreements that entered into force in 2002 (Bilateral I). Particular attention is paid to the institutional arrangements and their ability to adapt the agreements to new legal and political developments in the EU, the impact of the agreements on the functioning of Swiss democracy and how the Swiss political system affects the implementation of the bilateral sectoral agreements. In the process of carrying out this study, the authors conducted more than 20 personal interviews with EU and Swiss officials and experts between July and October 2005.

The study starts with a brief historical overview of EU-Swiss relations and the Swiss political system. Understanding the Swiss political system is essential to any analysis of relations between the EU and Switzerland. The second chapter therefore set out the constitutional framework of Switzerland. This is followed by an overview of the bilateral agreements concluded between Switzerland and the EU. The fourth chapter analyses the functioning of the bilateral sectoral agreements, focusing in particular on the implementation of Bilateral I. The fifth chapter compares EU-Swiss relations with the experiences of the EEA, the only arrangement for integration without membership that is more extensive than the Swiss model. The sixth and final chapter looks at the future of EU-Swiss relations, assesses possible measures to improve the functioning of the bilateral approach and, in light of the continuous development of the EU, suggests potential alternatives to the bilateral sectoral approach that currently characterises the relationship between Switzerland and the EU.

2. EU-Swiss relations and the Swiss political system

2.1 The development of EU-Swiss relations

The preservation of neutrality was the principal goal of Swiss foreign policy when the process of European integration was launched after World War II. Swiss policy towards European integration predates the establishment of the European Coal and Steel Community (ECSC) in the early 1950s, which was the precursor of today's EU. The official position of Switzerland can be traced back to 1947, when the Federal Council set out the principles for Swiss accession to the Organisation for European Economic Cooperation (OEEC, later the OECD).[2] The OEEC, created in 1948 to develop a joint European recovery programme and supervise the distribution of aid, emerged from the Marshall Plan, with Switzerland among its founding members.

A corollary of this goal was a fundamental rejection of surrendering any sovereignty that could damage the credibility of the policy of neutrality. This position remained basically unchanged until the end of the Cold War. The comprehensive 1988 report by the Federal Council on Swiss relations with the European Community (EC) emphasised the role of neutrality as an obstacle to Swiss membership in the EC. A further corollary was that Swiss foreign policy would be aimed towards the preservation of autonomy in economic and trade policy. A distinction was made between technical or economic organisations, in which Switzerland

---

[2] Goetchel (2004, p. 18).

could participate, and political and military organisations, which were regarded as incompatible with the principle of neutrality.

In line with these principles, the Swiss greeted the creation of the ECSC with a mixture of suspicion and support that has since guided the Swiss 'pragmatic middle-of-the-road' approach to European integration. Switzerland was deeply sceptical of positive political integration aimed at harmonisation and the development of common policies. It can be argued that as far as the European Economic Community (EEC) was concerned, the problem was thus initially not the substance of cooperation, but the ultimate political goals of European integration captured by the concept of an 'ever closer union'. Thus, the government ruled out participation in the ECSC, and later the EEC, primarily because of the stated goal of setting up a political European entity, which was seen as incompatible with the independence of the Swiss people.

On the other hand, the attempts to create a European free trade zone met with considerable interest and support in Switzerland, which was among the founding members of the European Free Trade Association (EFTA) in 1960. In accordance with the policy of favouring technical agreements and pragmatic solutions, a dialogue was soon established between Switzerland and the ECSC, leading to a first agreement in 1956 on transit of coal and steel through Switzerland and a consultation agreement between Switzerland and the ESCS High Authority (the precursor of the European Commission). Over the course of the next decades, these initial arrangements were followed by many bilateral sector-specific and mainly 'technical' agreements (see Chapter 3). Among these, the agreement of 1972, which mainly focused on trade in industrial goods, was until recently by far the most important agreement between Switzerland and the EU. Strongly supported by the Swiss people (72.5% voted in favour in a referendum), the 1972 agreement represented a compromise between entry together with its EFTA partners Britain and Denmark and standing on the sidelines of the integration process underway in Europe. Virtually identical agreements between other EFTA members and the EEC were negotiated in parallel, the main purpose of which was to reverse trade diversions caused by the creation of the Common Market. However, in spite of the accession of two EFTA partners in 1973, the possibility of accession was not seriously contemplated in Switzerland.

In 1984, the EC and EFTA launched the so-called 'Luxembourg process' aimed at deepening and broadening the 1972 agreements to also include services and non-tariff barriers, which were introduced into international trade agreements by the GATT Tokyo Round in the late 1970s. The launch of the plans for a Single European Market in 1985 added urgency to this process, as did the growing problems of the Swiss economy from the end of the 1980s. The process leading up to the European Economic Area (EEA) of today was initiated following the speech of then Commission President Jacques Delors to the European Parliament in January 1989, in which he called for the creation of a 'common European economic space' between the EC and EFTA, partly for the benefit of an expanded single market, but perhaps more importantly to avoid membership applications from the EFTA states.

Although Switzerland favoured bilateral as opposed to multilateral cooperation with the EC and was initially lukewarm towards the EC-EFTA economic space, it participated in the EEA negotiations from the beginning. Indeed, taking Swiss peculiarities into account was an important element in the EEA negotiations.[3] The Federal Council made clear that the successful conclusion of EEA negotiations depended upon Switzerland being guaranteed the continuation of direct democracy and federalism in Switzerland. The prospect of EEA participation required a considerable effort to adapt Swiss laws and regulations to those of the EU. This was undertaken under the law introduced in 1992 known as 'Eurolex', which requires all new Swiss legislation to be compatible with EC legislation.

But as the EEA negotiations proceeded, the EEA was increasingly regarded as a stepping-stone towards full EC accession. Between 1989 and 1992, five of the six EFTA states applied for full membership. Switzerland applied for EC membership on 20 May 1992, just a few weeks after the signing of the EEA agreement. It has been argued that dissatisfaction with the lack of an equal share in decision-making in the EEA led to the Swiss membership application, although broader geopolitical developments certainly played a role. The preservation of neutrality had been the principal argument against Swiss membership since the very beginning of European integration. The end of the Cold War and the subsequent accession of three neutral states to the EU in 1995 reduced this argument to the point of irrelevance. The 1999 Integration Report of the Swiss government concluded that "there is no doubt that EU membership is

---

[3] Sverdrup & Kux (1997, p. 7).

legally compatible with the status of permanent neutrality". It further argued that if the EU were to agree on a common defence and a new security structure, neutrality "might become meaningless".

In accordance with the Swiss Constitution, the EEA Treaty was submitted to a referendum on 6 December 1992. The EEA was rejected by the Swiss people in a close vote, with 49.7% voting in favour of the EEA and with a majority of the cantons voting against. It has been argued that this vote should be interpreted as a vote against full membership rather than the EEA as such, coming as it did only five months after the Swiss application for membership.[4] The membership application was suspended indefinitely following the EEA referendum. Several popular initiatives to re-launch negotiations on membership were made in the years following the 'no' vote on the EEA, but all where eventually rejected or abandoned. The Council of States – the second chamber of the Swiss parliament – rejected one such initiative in June 1996, while a similar proposal was rejected by almost 74% of the voters in a referendum in June 1997. Opposition was even higher to the most recent popular initiative to 'de-freeze' the Swiss membership application and resume accession negotiations, when 77% voted against the 'Yes to Europe' initiative on 4 March 2001. All cantons voted against resuming membership negotiations in both referenda.

Following the Swiss 'no' to the EEA, the Swiss government launched an economic revitalisation programme and in early February 1993 presented its proposals for negotiations of bilateral sectoral agreements in 15 areas.[5] The Swiss government decided that sector-by-sector agreements, the approach previously pursued in EC-Swiss relations, was the best way forward in the short-term, while keeping the option open of full membership in the longer-term. The EU agreed internally on its counter-proposals in November 1993 which called for negotiations to commence in

---

[4] Church (2000, p. 12).

[5] Namely, 1) Technical barriers to trade; 2) Public procurement; 3) Research; 4) Road transport; 5) Animal and plant protection legislation; 6) Air traffic; 7) Intellectual property, including labels of origins and geographic designations; 8) Processed agricultural goods; 9) Statistics; 10) Audio-visual sector; 11) Education, training and youth; 12) Outward processing of textiles; 14) Country of origin; and 15) Product liability.

four areas – road transport, research, market access for agricultural products and the free movement of persons – only the first two of which were on the Swiss list. The EU Council also called for talks on agreements on technical barriers to trade and public procurement. The EU Council further insisted on 'appropriate parallelism' as guiding criteria for the conclusion of the set of agreements. All of the agreements were seen as part of one package by the EU, and as a consequence, it insisted that all agreements must be adopted, enter into force and eventually expire simultaneously. But according to the Swiss Integration Bureau, the EU was unwilling to agree to a Swiss proposal of creating legal ties between the Bilateral I agreements and previous EU-Swiss agreements such as the 1972 agreement and the 1985 research agreement.

Negotiations on Bilateral I were launched in December 1994. The package included seven proposed agreements: the six suggested by the EU Council in November 1993 as well as an agreement on air transport. The agreements on free movement of persons and land transport were the most difficult areas in the negotiations. In the latter case this concerned in particular transit through the Swiss Alps, which was complicated by the Swiss Alps initiative supported in a referendum in 1994, which held up negotiations on Bilateral I for a period. The negotiations on Bilateral I were concluded at the political level in December 1998 following four years of negotiations, and the agreements were subsequently signed in Luxembourg on 21 June 1999. Switzerland formally ratified the seven agreements in October 2000, following the 67.2 % vote (and a majority in all cantons except two) in favour in a referendum held on 21 May and the almost unanimous support from the two houses of parliament (183 for and 11 against in the Federal Assembly and unanimous support in the Council of States). The EU ratification process was finalised in early 2002, allowing the seven agreements of Bilateral I to enter into force on 1 June 2002, nine and a half years after the Swiss people rejected the EEA agreement.

The EU and Switzerland had launched negotiations on a set of new sectoral bilateral agreements, known as Bilateral II, even before the entry into force of Bilateral I. The EU was initially reluctant to enter into another round of negotiations before Bilateral I was concluded. But concerns about possible Swiss violations of EU customs rules related to the smuggling of cigarettes and the development of an EU savings tax directive, for which some member states demanded bilateral agreements with Switzerland and other countries with favourable savings tax regimes, changed the EU's willingness to consider a new round of negotiations. Negotiations were launched in four areas – customs fraud, processed agricultural products, environment and statistics – in June 2001, followed by the start of negotiations in an additional seven areas – savings tax, Schengen, Dublin, services, media, pensions, and education, training and youth – in 2002.

The Bilateral II package thus consisted initially of 11 dossiers, seven of which were the so-called 'leftovers', areas in which Switzerland originally sought an agreement but which the EU did not agree to include in Bilateral I. In addition, Switzerland also sought an agreement on Schengen and Dublin, while the EU sought agreements in two areas – the fight against fraud and taxation of savings – not included in the original Swiss list. Switzerland further agreed in autumn 2003 to make a financial contribution to social and economic cohesion in the enlarged EU, modelled on the significantly increased contribution agreed between the EU and the other EFTA states. This contribution was according to some EU officials regarded as a necessary quid pro quo for Swiss association with the Schengen and Dublin agreements. Due to limited progress in the negotiations on the agreement on services, with a large number of outstanding issues, it was agreed in March 2003 to suspend negotiations, and that such an agreement would be completed at a later stage.

The (by then) ten agreements of Bilateral II were initialled at the first-ever EU-Swiss summit in May 2004, and were subsequently signed in October 2004. Most of the agreements in this package are as of early 2006 in the process of ratification. Three agreements – the agreement on processed agricultural products, the savings tax agreement and the agreement on pensions – have already entered into force. While none of the agreements of Bilateral II met the requirement for a compulsory referendum in Switzerland (see Chapter 2), seven of the eight agreements were submitted to an optional referendum in accordance with Art. 141 of the Swiss Constitution.[6] However, the only successful request for an optional referendum concerned the Schengen and Dublin agreements, which were subsequently approved by the Swiss people in a referendum on 5 June 2005, with 54.6% voting in favour.

---

[6] The agreement on processed agricultural goods was the only agreement that did not meet the constitutional requirement for an optional referendum, as it is only an adaptation of a protocol of the 1972 free trade agreement (see Chapter 3).

The EU enlargement in May 2004 had a direct impact on the EU-Swiss bilateral agreements. On 6 May 2004, the Commission formally requested an extension of Bilateral I to the new EU members. Six of the seven agreements were automatically extended. On the seventh – the agreement on the free movement of persons – a separate protocol extending the agreement to the new member states was negotiated from July 2003. The resulting protocol was approved in an optional referendum on 25 September 2005, with the extension of the agreement on free movement of persons approved by 56% of the voters.

After the referendum, the key issues in the Swiss European debate are concerned with the entry into force and subsequent full implementation of Bilaterals I and II, the possibility of concluding an overarching association agreement as well as further bilateral sectoral agreements, and finally the question whether the frozen application should be formally withdrawn, although no activation is expected during the current national parliamentary period (2003-07).

2.2   The Swiss constitutional framework

The bilateral sectoral approach and the implementation of the recently concluded agreements between Switzerland and the EU is highly influenced by Swiss structures of direct democracy, the principles of federalism and decentralisation as well as by Swiss administrative procedures. In order to understand national decision and legislation processes of relevance to the EU-Swiss bilateral agreements, this section highlights the main constitutional principles of the Swiss Confederation and the procedure for the conclusion of treaties.

2.2.1   The democratic principle

Switzerland is one of the oldest democracies in the world. Having been surrounded by monarchies and non-democratic entities for centuries, the democratic principle has become a factor of identification for the Swiss citizen and a constitutive element of the Swiss 'idea' and the Swiss Confederation. The identification factor has even been amplified in recent years in the debate on European integration and the possibility of Swiss accession to the European Union.

The most unique feature of Swiss democracy is that the people not only elect their representatives in parliament, but also decide on substantive matters through direct democracy. Although the democratic principle is of the utmost importance to the governance of Switzerland, it is not explicitly mentioned in the Swiss Constitution. It is, however, indirectly embodied in diverse provisions of the Constitution.

Art. 148 (1) of the Swiss Constitution emphasises that, subject to the rights of the people and the cantons, the federal assembly is the highest authority of the confederation. The election of the representatives in the two chambers of the parliament reflects the representative democracy as it exists in many different democratic nations.

The importance of the democratic principle is also shown by minimum requirements for the democratic organisation of the cantons. According to Art. 51 (1) of the Constitution, each canton has to adopt a democratic constitution on its own, which shall be approved by the confederation to assure its conformity with federal law (Art. 51 (2)). The Swiss Constitution on the other hand has to be approved by the people and can be revised by popular initiative.

Another significant outflow of the strongly highlighted principle of democracy is provided in Art. 190 of the Constitution: The federal court is not competent to declare on the compatibility of federal statutes and the Constitution, because the people's democratic legitimacy is considered higher than the court's legitimacy.

The Swiss Constitution provides for two mechanisms of direct democracy at the federal level: the Popular Initiative (Art. 138) and the Referendum (Arts 140 and 141). The Popular Initiative entails the right of citizens to propose a total or partial revision of the Swiss Constitution. The Referendum on the other hand entitles the people to vote on parliamentary decisions after the event. The referendum is similar to a veto of the people and is therefore both a safeguard and a delaying element in the political processes in Switzerland.

The Swiss democratic structures have been frequently discussed within the country in recent years, in particular whether the instruments of direct democracy allow Switzerland to be governed effectively and adapt to the fast-moving processes of European integration and globalisation.

2.2.2   The federal principle

Switzerland is a federal state. The cantons and their citizens constitute the fundamental elements of the Swiss Confederation. According to Art. 1 of the Constitution, "The Swiss people and the Cantons of Zürich, Berne, Lucerne, [...] form the Swiss Confederation".[7] But Swiss federalism differs from other federations. Unlike the federalism of the United States, Swiss federalism is not just an instrument to ensure the separation of powers, but is based on a constitutionally guaranteed balance between shared rule and self-rule: the powers are split up between the entities and the confederation (self-rule) and at the same time, the entities participate in the decision-making of the confederation (shared-rule). The speciality of Swiss federalism is that the federal level can only act in the area of expressly enumerated powers. The Constitution therefore transfers certain powers to the federal level while residuary powers lie with the cantons.[8]

Just like the democratic principle, the federal principle as such is not explicitly mentioned in the Swiss Constitution. There are however a number of constitutional provisions embodying the federal principle, including provisions on the division of powers between the cantons and the federal state, the participation of the cantons in constitutional revisions and the bicameral system of the federal parliament.

The Swiss Confederation is organised in three different governmental levels: the federal, the cantonal and the municipal. The subordinate entities, both the cantonal and the municipal, are autonomous in certain areas. As far as is possible, these entities are in the position to make their own decisions, taking into account their regional or local specificities.

The Constitution assigns most powers to the federal level and is, unlike the cantonal power, the highest authority of the three entities.[9] The autonomy of the cantons is therefore limited in the sense that they on the one hand have their own territory and citizen just like the classic 'state', but that their powers on the other hand are limited by the Swiss Constitution. According to Art. 3 of the Constitution they are "[...] sovereign insofar as their sovereignty is not limited by the Federal Constitution, they shall exercise all rights not transferred to the Confederation". Each canton has its

---

[7] While the 'Confederation' (der Bundesstaat) is the term for the Swiss federal state, the term 'federal' is used for the highest of the three governmental levels or entities (der Bund).

[8] Arts 3 and 42 of the Constitution.

[9] Also called the 'sovereignty' of the federation.

own institutions as well as cantonal authorities, organised freely within the framework of competences. The cantons of Switzerland are entitled to conclude treaties among themselves in the domains where they have remained sovereign, as long as such treaties do not harm the interests of the federation or other cantons (Art. 48). They are – again within the scope of their powers – even entitled to conclude treaties with foreign states (Art. 56).

The Swiss political system does not have an institutionalised representation of the cantons. The 46 members[10] of the Council of States (Ständerat) constitute the second chamber of the Swiss Parliament and politically represent the interests of the cantons of Switzerland in the Parliament. On the other hand, the governments of the cantons, involved in the different implementation aspects of treaties, are not represented in the Council of States.

The autonomy of the third entity – the municipalities – is guaranteed within the limits fixed by cantonal law (Art. 50). By virtue of cantonal law the municipalities are corporate bodies of public law entitled to fulfil local public tasks with significant autonomy.

In light of the deepening of EU-Swiss relations with Bilaterals I and II and the broader process of globalisation, the self-rule and the shared-rule of the cantons have become a topic of political debate in Switzerland. Although the principle itself has never been questioned as such, federalism is one of the discussed topics in the confederation. Previous versions of the Swiss Constitution provided a more extensive autonomy to the cantons. The self-rule principle of the cantons was curtailed as a result of internationalisation and the increasing extension of federal powers and the connected changes in legislative procedures. Due to the political interdependence of the confederation and the cantons, there has hardly remained one item where the cantons are fully autonomous. In many policy fields today, there is a rather complex meshing of cantonal and federal law.

---

[10] The cantons of Obwalden and Nidwalden, Basel-City and Basel-Country, Appenzell outer Rhodes and Appenzell Inner Rhodes select one representative each, while the other cantons (ranging in size from Zürich with over 1 million inhabitants to Uri with roughly 36,000 inhabitants) select two senators.

The implications for the cantons of the bilateral agreements with the EU are not limited to the specific policy dossiers in which they have extensive powers that are covered in the agreements. One of the main tasks of the cantons is the implementation of federal legislation and objectives (Art. 46), and many, if not most, of the sectors of the bilateral agreements have an impact on these implementation tasks of the cantons. This cantonal challenge reveals and clarifies their interest in timely and extensive consultations with the federal government. In the course of negotiating and implementing the bilateral agreements, it was therefore very important to establish a formal procedure to accommodate the interests of the cantons. Those consultation rights of the cantons in legislation procedures have now been improved and introduced in the revised Constitution of 1999 (see Chapter 4.2.4.).

2.2.3   The neutrality principle

Switzerland had an old tradition of conducting warfare and providing mercenary services on behalf of other countries. But when the Thirty Year's War (1618-1648) threatened the political unity of Catholic and Protestant cantons, a policy of neutrality was adopted for the first time. Following the Napoleonic Wars, the neutrality of Switzerland was recognised in the Treaty of Paris of 1815, and has been reaffirmed several times since then.

The implications of Swiss neutrality in operational policy terms have been adjusted regularly over the course of time. Switzerland abides by a concept of active neutrality through which perpetual, armed neutrality shall be preserved. Switzerland will not initiate a war or take part in any military aggression. Furthermore, Switzerland remains neutral in all wars, independent of the parties involved and does not support any of the parties in the conflict. At the same time, Switzerland's active foreign policy is based on solidarity and participation. The goals of this concept are enumerated in the Constitution: according to Art. 54 (3) the "Confederation shall contribute to [...] promote respect for human rights, democracy, the peaceful coexistence of nations [...]".

Whereas Switzerland was a founding member of the League of Nations after World War 1, Switzerland did not become a member of the United Nations until 18 July 2002, even though the UN has numerous agencies located in Geneva, and despite the fact that neutrality was not an obstacle for UN membership of other neutral states such as Austria, Sweden, Finland and Ireland a long time ago. The accession of Switzerland to the United Nations (UN) and the debate that followed the accession procedure have shown that Swiss neutrality is not affected by its accession to the UN. This was also declared by the Federal Council in 2000, requiring that the Federal Council's application for accession should point out the neutrality of Switzerland and that this should be repeated on the occasion of the first General Assembly of the UN.[11] With its accession to the UN, Switzerland entered an organisation of collective security under conditions that do not compromise its neutrality policy. Switzerland will for example contribute financially to peacekeeping operations by the UN, but it is not obliged to commit troops for this purpose.

Nevertheless, Switzerland's long tradition of self-rule, autonomy and independence in foreign policy has a psychological impact on the general attitude of the population towards European integration processes.

2.3 The conclusion of international treaties

2.3.1 *Constitutional basis*

According to Art. 54 of the Swiss Constitution, the conclusion of treaties is principally a federal matter, even if the subject matter falls within the scope of cantonal powers (such as police or education).[12] The cantons participate in the preparation of foreign policy decisions which concern their powers or their essential interests (Art. 55 (1)). Although foreign relations are a federal matter, the cantons have an additional competence for the conclusion of treaties with foreign countries, but only within the scope of their powers. Those cantonal treaties may of course not be contrary to the law or to the interests of the federation (Art. 56). The federal assembly does not participate in the negotiation of international agreements, but must according to Art. 166 (1) be consulted.

2.3.2 *Procedures for the conclusion of international treaties*

According to the Constitution, the Federal Council conducts foreign relations, including the negotiation of international agreements. It

---

[11] "Botschaft" of the Federal Council on the popular initiative on the accession of Switzerland to the United Nations, 4 December 2000, p. 1212 ff.

[12] Müller (2001).

nominates and instructs the Swiss delegation and grants authorisation to the members of the delegation to sign the negotiated treaty.[13]

An international agreement negotiated by the executive needs the approval of the Federal Assembly. The assembly is only in a position to accept or to reject the treaty, and cannot submit any modification proposals (Arts 166 (2) and 184 (2)). Although the approval of the Parliament is the general rule, the Constitution provides some significant exceptions based on statute or international law, empowering the Federal Council to conclude treaties independently (Art. 166 (2)).[14] Those exceptions were introduced in the Federal Statute on the Organisation of the Government and Administration (RVOG).[15] According to its Art. 7, the Federal Council is empowered to conclude treaties without the approval of the assembly if:

- the treaty does not impose new duties on Switzerland or does not entail the waiving of such duties (Art. 7, a RVOG);

- the agreement is only of an executive nature (treaty on the execution of an existing agreement) (Art. 7, b RVOG);

- the subject of the treaty is in the exclusive power of the Federal Council (Art. 7, c RVOG); and

- the treaty regulates administrative and technical matters of limited importance (so-called 'bagatelle treaties'). These kinds of treaties primarily affect the public administration, do not require any statute law adaptations, do not affect the interest of the individual and do not generate significant expenses. Furthermore the treaty shall be susceptible to termination on short notice[16] (Art. 7, d RVOG).

The democratic rights of the *Mandatory Treaty Referendum* (Art. 140 (2) b) and the *Optional Treaty Referendum* (Art. 141 (1) d) have a direct bearing on the procedure for the conclusion of international treaties. Such treaties are subject to a Mandatory Treaty Referendum if they entail entry into 1)

---

[13] Häfelin & Haller (2001). The Federal Council represents Switzerland abroad with respect to the participatory rights of the Federal Parliament (Art. 184 of the Constitution).

[14] Müller (2001, §70, N 38). See also Chapter 2.6 of the present work.

[15] Regierungs- und Verwaltungsorganisationsgesetz vom 21. März 1997, RVOG, SR 172.010.

[16] Häfelin & Haller (2001, N 1901).

organisations for collective security, such as the Swiss accession to the UN in 2002, or 2) supranational communities such as the EU. In either of these two circumstances, the accession treaty shall be submitted to the vote of the people *and* the cantons.[17] In other words, the entry into such organisations/supranational communities needs two separate majorities; the majority of the people *and* the majority of the cantons.[18]There have been many examples in the history of Switzerland where the majority of the cantons seemed to be the problematic and final factor for a vote.

International treaties are subject to Optional Treaty Referenda if they are 1) of unlimited duration and may not be terminated, 2) provide for the entry into an international organisation and 3) involve a multilateral unification of law, such as the bilateral agreements between the Swiss Confederation and the European Union or the European Convention on Human Rights. These referenda are 'optional' in the sense that 50,000 Swiss citizens or eight cantons are entitled to request a referendum in order to submit a treaty of this category to the vote of the people.[19] The vote on an Optional Treaty Referendum does not need the majority of the cantons, unlike the Mandatory Treaty Referendum.

After the approval by the Federal Assembly and a possible positive referendum, ratification falls within the power of the Federal Council (Art. 184 (2)). Unlike other states such as the UK or the Nordic countries, which have adopted a so-called 'dualistic system', Switzerland has adopted the monistic system in connection with treaties: Further transformation into national law is therefore not required. An international treaty concluded by Switzerland does not gain binding force for individuals until its publication in the Official Register of Federal Law (Amtliche Sammlung des Bundesrechts-AS).[20]

---

[17] Although the EEA entails supranational elements but does not provide any 'supranational community' in terms of Art. 140 (2) b of the Constitution, the decree on the EEA of 9 October 1992, was treated like a constitutional revision and was therefore submitted to the vote of the people and the cantons; See BBl 1992 IV 538.

[18] As it has to be a majority, the positive vote needs the majority of 12 cantons. According to Art. 142 (4) of the constitution the 'half-cantons' are counted half.

[19] Müller (2001, N 44 ff).

[20] Arts 2 and 10 of the Federal Publication Act, SR 170.512; see also Häfelin & Haller (2001, N 1914 ff).

3. The bilateral agreements between the EU and Switzerland

No other third country has entered into as many agreements with the EU as has Switzerland. Indeed, it is difficult to determine the precise number of bilateral agreements, as they vary according to the sources and their definition of what should be understood as an 'agreement'. Some experts claim that more than 100 agreements have been concluded over the last 30 years.[21] This very high number is achieved by counting the numerous amendments and updates to the various agreements as separate agreements, and the actual number of agreements is substantially lower. This chapter sets out the scope of the agreements concluded between Switzerland and the EU since the creation of the European Coal and Steel Community (ECSC), the precursor to the EU some fifty years ago, focusing on Bilaterals I and II.

3.1 Earlier agreements

Contractual relations between Switzerland and the European Communities were first established in the late 1950s, with a consultation agreement between the Swiss federal government and the High Authority of the ECSC, and an agreement on transit of coal and steel by railway through Switzerland. In the subsequent four decades, a series of (mainly limited and sectoral) agreements were concluded between the two sides. The 25 agreements reached between the EU and Switzerland since the creation of the ECSC and that are not part of Bilaterals I and II are listed in Box 1.

---

[21] Hewitt Associates (2002).

Box 1. Agreements between Switzerland and the EU, 1956-2004

Trade and industry agreements

1967   Tariffs on certain cheeses
1972   Agreement between the EC and Switzerland (the 'free trade agreement')*
1974   Clock and watch industry
1985   Trade in soups, sauces and condiments
1986   Trade in non-agricultural and processed agricultural goods
1989   Trade in electronic data interchange systems
1990   Simplification of inspections and formalities in respect to the carriage of goods
1995   Trade in certain agricultural and fishery products
2001   Tariff preferences under the General System of Preferences (GSP)

Transport agreements

1956   Railway tariffs for the carriage of coal and steel through Swiss territory
1992   Carriage of goods by road and rail

Research agreements

1978   Thermonuclear fusion and plasma physics
1985   Scientific and technical cooperation
1988   R&D in the field of wood, including cork, as a renewable raw material
1988   R&D in the field of advanced materials (Euram)
1991   European Stimulation Plan for the Economic Sciences (SPES)
1991   EEC R&D programme in the field of applied metrology and chemical analysis

Other bilateral agreements

1957   Consultation agreement between Switzerland and the ECSC High Authority
1984   Prevention of fraud
1988   Terminology
1991   Direct insurance other than life insurance
2004   Europol

Multilateral agreements: EEC/EFTA conventions

1987   On the simplification of formalities on trade in goods
1987   On a common transit procedure
1990   Procedure for the exchange of information in the field of technical regulations

---

* The 1972 agreement (formally consisting of two agreements, one with the European Community and one with the ECSC) is frequently referred to as the 'free trade agreement', despite the fact that there is no reference to free trade in the title. Hereafter, it is referred to as the 1972 agreement.

Source: European Commission.

Most of these are bilateral agreements between Switzerland and the EU, but the list also includes multilateral agreements of particular relevance to EU-Swiss relations concluded between the EEC and its member states on the one hand, and the EFTA member states on the other.

Most of these are traditional international cooperation agreements in areas such as trade and research, and the scope of each agreement is limited, with agreements on single products and narrowly defined sectors, for instance the agreements on trade in cheese, the clock and watch industry, cooperation on fusion research and fraud. Several of these agreements have been changed since then. The 1972 agreement has for instance been amended more than a dozen times since it was first concluded, in certain cases through the adoption of additional protocols that arguably had greater implications for the bilateral relationship than many of the other, more limited agreements. Some of these agreements were superseded by Bilaterals I and II, for instance agreements in the fields of research, transport and trade.

Until the conclusion of Bilateral I, the 1972 agreement was the principal bilateral agreement between Switzerland and the European Community. Negotiated in parallel with similar agreements between the EC the other EFTA states, the 1972 agreement provides for free trade in industrial products. The EU and Switzerland have also negotiated other agreements in parallel with the bilateral packages, most notably the cooperation agreement with the European Police Office (Europol) signed in September 2004.

3.2   Bilateral I

The first set of bilateral agreements negotiated between 1994 and 1998 consists of seven agreements.

Box 2. Bilateral I sectoral agreements

1. Research
2. Technical barriers to trade
3. Free movement of persons
4. Air transport
5. Land transport
6. Agriculture
7. Public procurement

3.2.1 Research

Cooperation on research between Switzerland and the EC/EU has a long history. A number of agreements were concluded from the 1970s onwards, in specific areas (for instance wood as a renewable material, thermonuclear physics, metrology), as well as a broader agreement on scientific cooperation in 1985-86, which allowed for limited Swiss participation in certain EC research programmes on a project-by-project basis, fully and directly financed by the Swiss government. The funds allocated to this were steadily increased, from 11 million Swiss francs (CHF) in 1992 to 120 million CHF (approximately €80 million) in 2002, funding Swiss participation in more than 1,400 projects.

The research agreement concluded as part of the Bilateral I package represents a considerable upgrade of the 1985 agreement, making Switzerland one of five 'associated states' (the others are the other EFTA member states and Israel) of the EU's 5th Framework Programmes on Research. This status grants Swiss research establishments equal rights in all programmes and activities of the on-going framework programme. More specifically, researchers in associate states have the same rights and obligations as researchers from EU member states, including the right to assume the role of project coordinator, and receive their funding from the Commission in accordance with EU rules. For example, in shared-cost projects, Swiss institutions need find only one partner from a member state to form a consortium. Previous restrictions, such as on Marie Curie actions or CRAFT projects, do not apply. Switzerland's participation in future EU framework programmes on research requires negotiations on renewal of the research agreement.

3.2.2 Technical barriers to trade

This agreement provides for mutual recognition of conformity assessments of standards (certificates, tests, product authorisations, etc.) across a wide range of industrial products.[22] The agreement recognises the equivalence of

---

[22] More than a dozen product groups are listed: Machines; medical products; manufacturing checks for pharmaceuticals (although authorisation for the sale of medicine is not covered); testing for the registration of chemical substances; toys; construction machines; motor vehicles, tractors; telecommunications installations; measurement instruments; gas heating boilers and appliances; electrical and

Swiss legislation with that of the EU, which simplifies procedures and reduces costs for producers in both markets. Only one single test of conformity will henceforth be required for a product covered by this agreement to be acceptable in both Swiss and EU markets.

However, merchandise from third countries may not be certified in accordance with standards by Swiss bodies for the purpose of commercialisation in the EU. In areas not covered by the agreements and where Swiss and EU requirements differ, for instance, certain chemical substances, phytosanitary products, biocides and construction products, two conformity tests will still be required, although it is now possible for both tests to be undertaken by Swiss authorities.

3.2.3   Free movement of persons

This is widely seen as the most important agreement in the Bilateral I package. The agreement sets out a progressive opening of the labour market leading eventually to the free movement of persons between Switzerland and the EU. Swiss and EU nationals will be entitled to the same working and living conditions in Switzerland and the EU.

The agreement covers workers of all kinds, including the self-employed and the unemployed given that they have sufficient financial means of their own. The agreement also includes the mutual recognition of professional diplomas and coordination of social insurance. Switzerland is incorporated into the multilateral EU social security totalisation agreement, which covers pensions, health care, family allowances and other social security benefits. Employers remain covered for pensions by their home country, whereas health care, sickness, workers' compensation, etc. are covered by the host country. The agreement also covers cross-border provisions of services for shorter periods.

3.2.4   Air transport

This agreement provides for Switzerland to be included in the EU's civil aviation market. The *acquis communautaire* in this field is extended to

---

electromagnetic compatibility appliances; equipment used in environments where there is a high risk of explosion; equipment for the protection of individuals; and pressure vessels.

Switzerland, and Swiss airlines are given equal access to the EU's deregulated market on a reciprocal basis. Swiss companies are granted commercial flying rights, are included in a ban on discrimination on the basis of nationality and are extended the right to acquire a majority stake in EU airlines. Restrictions on supply and sales are removed, and Swiss airlines can serve any destination, with planes of any capacity.

The agreement opens up the possibility of levying fees on noise and other environmentally related issues, including restrictions on landing rights, if it is done in a non-discriminatory fashion. The air transport agreement replaces more than a dozen less extensive bilateral agreements with EU member states on civil aviation.

3.2.5   Land transport

The agreement calls for the coordination of transport policy, and sets out a gradual reciprocal opening of markets for the transport of goods and people by road and rail between Switzerland and the EU. The agreement allows for 'grand cabotage' (transport between two EU member states), subject to certain temporary restrictions, while regular cabotage (transport within a member state) is excluded from the agreement.

The agreement increases the maximum weight of heavy goods vehicles (HGVs) allowed to transit Switzerland from 28 tonnes before the agreement was negotiated to 40 tonnes in 2005. To compensate and encourage a shift in traffic from road to rail, the agreement envisages a significant increase in the HGV tax for transit through Switzerland. Other restrictions, such as the ban of HGV travel on Sundays and at night, will remain.

Both sides also commit themselves to improve the railway infrastructure. Switzerland undertakes to build the tunnels planned under the New Transalpine Railways (NEAT) at a cost of more than €10 billion, while the EU is committed to improve access both to the north and south of NEAT. The land transport agreement replaces previous transport agreements between Switzerland and the EU, as well as bilateral agreements with most member states. Some of the latter include barriers to trade such as quotas, which will now be removed.

3.2.6   Agriculture

This agreement liberalises trade in certain categories of agricultural products by lowering tariffs and reducing or eliminating a number of non-tariff barriers.

The agreement grants better access to the other's markets, in particular on products of special interest to one or the other party. A number of reciprocal concessions were made over fruit and vegetables, horticultural products and to a lesser extent, dried meats and wine specialties. Tariffs will be reduced on products like cheese, fruit and vegetables where Switzerland is competitive. Switzerland on the other side has made financial concessions on fruits and vegetables in the winter season, and for products not grown in Switzerland. A number of important agricultural products such as meat, wheat and milk are not subject to tariff reductions under this agreement.

Mutual recognition of technical specifications is extended to pesticides, animal feeds, seeds, biological agriculture, rules for the sale of wine and, to some extent, veterinary medicine, and quality standards for fruit and vegetables. Switzerland has been granted the responsibility by the EU of certification on Swiss territory, on the basis of EU rules, of fruit and vegetables for export. Added to the agreement was a joint statement that mutual protection of labels guaranteeing the origins of products and so-called 'protected geographical indications' such as champagne and feta cheese – one of the 15 items on the Swiss 'wish-list' of February 1993 – would be incorporated in the agreement in the future.

3.2.7   Public procurement

The EU-Swiss agreement on public procurement builds on the WTO agreement on public procurement markets (APM). This multilateral agreement introduced rules on tenders issued by national and regional authorities in the areas of water, public transport, energy and construction (with certain limits) based on the principals of equal treatment (non-discrimination), transparent procedures, and the right of legal appeal on tenders and contracts (of a certain size).

The bilateral agreement on public procurement extends beyond the scope of the APM into the fields of telecommunications and rail transport, broadens the coverage to the entire energy sector (i.e. gas, oil and coal in addition to electricity) and also includes procurement by local governments and private companies.

3.3 Bilateral II

The second set of bilateral sectoral agreements negotiated between 2001 and 2004 consists of nine agreements and one declaration of intent.

Box 3. Bilateral II sectoral agreement

1.   Processed agricultural goods
2.   Statistics
3.   Media
4.   Environment
5.   Pensions
6.   Education, occupational training, youth (declaration of intent)
7.   Taxation of savings
8.   Schengen
9.   Dublin
10. Fight against fraud

3.3.1 Processed agricultural products

This agreement further liberalises trade in processed agricultural goods, which were only partially included in the 1972 agreement. Protocol 2 of the 1972 agreement, which was adopted in 1977, removed duties on the industrial component of such goods, with a price compensation mechanism of duties and export subsidies introduced for the raw material aspects of the products, to take account of the disadvantage of high price differences on certain basic agricultural goods.

The agreement on processed agricultural products amends and improves Protocol 2 of the 1972 agreement, by simplifying the price compensation scheme and by extending the scope of application of the agreement. The principle of net price compensation is introduced to simplify procedures. In accordance with Protocol 2 of the 1972 agreement, world prices were used as the starting point to calculate the price compensation. With the agreement on processed agricultural products, the much smaller differences between Swiss and EU prices will be used as the reference.

As prices are higher in Switzerland, the consequence of the net price compensation method is that duties and export subsidies on processed agricultural goods covered by the agreement are completely abolished on the EU side. In some areas Switzerland will also completely abolish duties and export contributions, affecting products such as coffee, cocoa, jams, mineral water, soft drinks, beer and spirits. In other areas, Switzerland will make a corresponding reduction in duties and reduce its export subsidies. This applies to products such as flour, dried milk, butter and vegetable fat, and has consequences across a wide range of products such as chocolate, pasta, biscuits, bread, pastries, ice cream and other processed foods.

Furthermore, the scope of application of the agreement has been widened to include additional products, notably those brought about as a result of technological advances made in the food industry since the 1970s, e.g. food supplements and phyto-pharmaceuticals.

3.3.2 Statistics

This agreement enables Switzerland to access pan-European data and guarantees the compatibility of data, as statistical data collection in Switzerland is brought in line with Eurostat (Statistical Office of the EC) standards. A joint annual programme for Switzerland and the EC is being developed within the framework of the EU's multi-year statistics programme.

3.3.3 Media

The MEDIA programme was established in 1991, to promote the creation and distribution of film productions in Europe and to establish a training programme for EU film industry professionals. Switzerland joined the MEDIA programme upon its creation in 1991, as the first non-EU member state. This participation was ended by the EU following the Swiss rejection of the EEA in December 1992.

The current (third generation) MEDIA programmes consist of two parts: Media Plus, which promotes creation and distribution of European films, and MEDIA Training Programmes. With the media agreement, the EU now funds Swiss-EU member state co-productions through Media Plus, and Swiss film makers qualify for the MEDIA Training Programmes.

3.3.4 Environment

This agreement allows Switzerland to join the European Environmental Agency, whose goals are to provide the EU with objective, reliable information on the state of the environment, provide advice to the EU on environmental policy and disseminate information to the public. An environmental information and observation network (EIONET) plays a key role in the work of the European Environmental Agency. While it was established as an EC agency, the European Environmental Agency also includes as members the candidate countries and the other EFTA member states. Switzerland currently cooperates with the European Environmental Agency on an informal basis, through selective participation in technical and scientific projects.

The agreement will allow Swiss institutions to participate in European Environmental Agency programmes and respond to invitations to tender from the European Environmental Agency. Switzerland will get full access to EIONET, to which it will contribute comparable environmental data, thus enabling Switzerland to be included in European-wide studies.

3.3.5   Pensions

The agreement on pensions was concluded to avoid double taxation of the pensions of former EU officials residing in Switzerland. As Bilateral I was concluded in 1999, it was agreed, at the behest of the EU, to include this issue in the Bilateral II negotiations. The agreement reached entails that Switzerland grants an income-tax exemption on income from pensions of retired EU officials living in Switzerland, provided that the income is taxed at source (i.e. in the EU). In contrast to the other agreements of Bilateral II, this is an agreement between the European Commission and the Swiss Federal Council and affects approximately 50 residents of Switzerland.

3.3.6   Education, occupational training, and youth

The Swiss rejection of membership in the European Economic Area made it impossible for the country to participate in EU programmes on education, such as SOCRATES II (general school and university education, including ERASMUS exchange programmes), LEONARDO DA VINCI II (professional training) and YOUTH (extra-curricular youth activities). From 1994 onwards, Switzerland adopted certain transitional financial measures that enabled it to participate as a 'tacit partner', including for instance in the ERASMUS programme. This participation was based on the goodwill of the EU, and not a contractual agreement between Switzerland and the EU, so Switzerland has sought an agreement with the EU. During the negotiations of Bilateral II, the two parties agreed on annual high-level meetings to strengthen the current cooperation in this area and to prepare talks on Swiss participation in the future.

3.3.7 Taxation of savings

This agreement came about as a result of the EU directive on savings tax, and was arguably the most politically sensitive agreement in the negotiations of Bilateral II. Three EU member states – Austria, Belgium and Luxembourg – were unwilling to accept the provisions on exchange of information, and introduced a withholding tax on savings instead. They further insisted that they would only agree to this if agreements on taxation of savings were concluded between the EU and Switzerland and other low-tax countries such as Andorra, Liechtenstein, Monaco and San Marino.

The core of the agreement is the obligation of Switzerland to introduce a retention tax on income from savings to natural persons domiciled for taxation purposes in the EU. Two-thirds of the income from the tax, set eventually at 35%, will be paid back to the EU member state. The agreement does not include legal persons, i.e. companies, and does not apply to interest payments on debtors residing in Switzerland. According to some EU officials, the latter provision ensures that the scope of application of the savings tax agreement will be very limited.

3.3.8 Schengen

The Schengen association agreement will lead to the eventual abolition of controls of persons on the border between the EU and Switzerland. Systematic random controls of persons at the frontier will be replaced by mobile controls within the country. The agreement allows for border controls to be re-introduced on special occasions in situations of particularly high risk (for instance high-level political meetings and sports events). As Switzerland is not part of the EU's customs union, control of goods at the EU-Swiss border will continue.

The Schengen association agreement includes a number of common measures to control the common external border, including a common visa policy for shorter stays, cross-border police cooperation and judicial cooperation in the area of criminal justice. The agreement gives Swiss authorities access to the Schengen Information System (SIS) computer network, which provides information of wanted or undesirable persons and is regarded as an important tool in the fight against cross-border crime, such as smuggling, trafficking, etc. The agreement further improves and facilitates mutual legal assistance in criminal matters, including on tax offences. The latter issue was one of the last to be resolved in the Bilateral II negotiations.

3.3.9 Dublin

The Dublin association agreement allows Switzerland to participate in EU asylum cooperation. The Dublin Convention sets out common rules for the proceedings of asylum seekers and gives access to the fingerprint-database Eurodac, which was established in January 2003. This allows double or multiple asylum applications to be identified in an easier and more transparent way. As the database is continuously expanded, the ability of the Swiss authorities to prevent so-called 'asylum shopping' is improved.

3.3.10 Fight against fraud

This agreement represents an upgrade of a protocol on cooperation against fraud to the 1972 free trade agreement between the EU and Switzerland. While this protocol had strengthened EU-Swiss cooperation against fraud, certain issues such as time-consuming legal processes and the absence of an agreement on extradition, were unresolved.

The agreement introduces a commitment to provide administrative and legal assistance on indirect taxes (customs duties, VAT, specific excise duties, etc.), subsidies and public procurement, and speeds up cooperation between customs, tax and judicial authorities. The scope of legal assistance is extended from tax fraud to tax offences relating to indirect taxes in the EU, although direct taxes are not covered by the agreement. Coercive measures are possible above certain limits. This was one of the last dossiers to be concluded in the Bilateral II negotiations.

3.4   Institutional framework of the bilateral agreements

3.4.1   Bilateral committees

As a general rule, each bilateral sectoral agreement between the EU and Switzerland is managed by a Joint or Mixed Committee.[23] These bodies are composed of representatives from the EU and Switzerland and make decisions by consensus.

There are some exceptions to this rule. First, such committees were only established to manage some of the older agreements, such as the 1972 agreement and the clock and watch agreement. In addition to the seven committees set up to manage Bilateral I, there are currently ten committees managing the pre-Bilateral I agreements. Bilateral committees will be established for all of the agreements of Bilateral II, with the exception of the pensions and savings tax agreements, for which there will be no committees as the agreements are 'static', and will in the latter case remain unchanged until a possible revision of the agreement will be discussed in 2013. The agreement on processed agricultural goods will be managed under the joint committee established for the management of the 1972 agreement. The agreements on agriculture are furthermore managed both by a Veterinary Committee and an Agriculture Committee. In some of these agreements, the joint committee is assisted by sub-committees of experts and lower level officials. There are for instance ten such sub-committees working on the agriculture agreement of Bilateral I. In total, 13 new joint committees will be established as a result of Bilaterals I and II.

The bilateral committees typically meet once per year, which is often the minimum required by the agreements. In other cases, for example in the agreement on environment, the Joint Committee will only meet upon the request of either of the parties (Art. 16 (1)), while in other agreements, the parties meet more often than once per year. Although each committee sets its own rules of procedure, the chairmanship of the committee, which includes the formal responsibility to set the agenda, typically rotates between the EU and the Swiss side. In practice, the agenda circulates back and forth between the two parties and is agreed beforehand, so that there

---

[23] Hereafter referred to as joint committees unless a specific committee with another name is discussed.

are few surprises in the statements and opinions expressed in the actual meetings of the various joint committees.

3.4.2 Composition of the bilateral committees

The joint committees are as a rule bilateral, with meetings between officials from the Swiss central administration and the European Commission. The members of the Swiss delegation are elected by the Federal Council. The standing members of the delegation consist of officials of the Federal Offices involved.[24] The cantons have a representative in the five committees governing agreements in which cantonal policy competences are relevant.[25] The Swiss delegation to the bilateral committees also includes a representative of the Swiss Integration Bureau and the Mission to the EU in Brussels. In most delegations there is also a representative of the Directorate of International Law of the Foreign Affairs Office.

Most EU agreements with third countries are managed by the Directorate General (DG) for External Relations of the European Commission. On the EU-Swiss agreements, the management of the joint committees is divided among the relevant sectoral DGs.[26] EU-Swiss relations here differ from most other EU relationships with third countries, in which DG External Relations plays the lead role on the EU side. In the Swiss case, DG External Relations is only responsible for the 1972 agreement and the agreement on free movement of persons, and could possibly be given responsibility also for the management of the Schengen and Dublin association agreements.

---

[24] For example in the joint committee for the agreement on the free movement of persons: Federal Migration Office, Federal Office for Education and Technology, Federal Office for Social Security and Federal Secretariat of Economy (Seco).

[25] These are the agreements on public procurement, air transport, overland transport and the free movement of persons in Bilateral I. In Bilateral II, the KdK is working on ensuring the canton's representation in the Schengen Mixed Committeee.

[26] For example DG Transport and Energy on the air and overland transport agreements, DG Health and Consumer Protection and DG Agriculture on the agriculture agreement, DG Environment on the environment agreement, etc.

3.4.3   Other committees

Several of the agreements entail Swiss participation in EU and EC programmes and agencies, and include provisions on the participation of Swiss representatives in the bodies of these programmes and agencies. As a result of the agreement on environment, for example, Swiss representatives will participate on the board of the European Environmental Agency to discuss environmental research projects without any formal voting powers. A unilateral declaration by the EU governs Swiss participation, without voting rights, in the panels that support the Commission in developing the statistics programme. On research, Switzerland has observer status in the overall FP6 programme committee and the programme committees for the thematic sub-headings of the programme in which Switzerland participates financially, where work programmes and tenders are discussed.

3.4.4   A special case: The Schengen Mixed Committee

The Mixed Committee of the Schengen association agreement differs from the typical joint committees in two ways. First, although there are formally two such Mixed Committees with associated states, one with Switzerland and the other with Iceland and Norway, the meetings are held together. It thus functions as a multilateral agreement, one of the very few such agreements between the EU and third countries. Secondly, the EU is represented in most international agreements by the so-called 'Troika', which is led by the EU presidency and assisted by the incoming chair of the EU Council, the secretariat of the Council and the European Commission, or, as in the case of the other EU-Swiss agreements, by the European Commission alone. By contrast, all member states participate in the Schengen Mixed Committee. In practice, this arrangement entails participation by non-member states in the EU's Council of Ministers and its important sub-groups, the COREPER and the working groups, as well as in the Commission's working groups responsible for the preparation and implementation of legislation alongside the member states. The associates participate in the discussions on an equal basis with the EU member states, but do not have a vote. The fact that decisions are usually made by consensus reduces the significance of the absence of a formal vote, even though the search for consensus does not have to extend to the associated partners.

3.4.5 Tasks of the bilateral committees

The main function of the bilateral committees is to ensure the proper implementation of the agreements, providing a forum for dialogue aimed at resolving misunderstandings and differences in interpretation of the provisions of the agreement. This includes the important task of integrating new legal provisions by adapting the agreements, as well as being the arena for the settlement of disputes between the two sides (see sections 3.5 and 3.6 below). Although the specific provisions of the tasks differ from one agreement to another, they are in practice quite similar.

The bilateral committees serve as the principal forum for the exchange of information concerning the development of the agreements. These discussions can cover the day-to-day implementation of the agreements, legislative developments in Switzerland and the EU, the effects of legal changes to the agreements and the effects of a new jurisdiction to the agreements.

3.5 Adapting the agreements to new legislation

Whether or not, or the extent to which, the bilateral sectoral agreements entail a commitment by Switzerland to adopt EU rules and standards, the (in)famous *acquis communautaire*, is arguably the most fundamental, controversial and complex question arising from Bilaterals I and II. The extent to which the various agreements should be based on the *acquis* was a recurring issue of disagreements between Swiss and EU officials in the negotiations of Bilaterals I and II, and was the main reason why the talks on an agreement on services was abandoned in 2003.

Swiss authorities go to great lengths to underline that most of the agreements in Bilaterals I and II take the form of 'traditional' agreements of international cooperation.[27] In many respects, this is correct. First, decisions on any changes to any of the agreements are made by consensus between the EU and Switzerland. Secondly, any dispute between the EU and Switzerland on any agreement, with one notable exception discussed below, will be settled bilaterally in the joint committees. Thirdly, each of the two parties is responsible for the proper implementation of the

---

[27] See for instance the explanatory documents for Bilaterals I and II on the homepage of the Swiss Integration Bureau (www.europa.admin.ch).

agreements on its own territory, again however with some notable exceptions that are discussed below.

The Swiss Integration Bureau distinguishes between three types of agreements in its analysis of Bilateral I: five deregulation agreements, one cooperation agreement and one 'partial integration' agreement, namely the agreement on air transport. Most of the agreements of Bilateral II are cooperation agreements. Several of these are essentially 'static' agreements, such as the agreement on the fight against fraud and on savings tax, in the sense that no changes to the provisions of the agreement are envisaged. On the other hand, most of the agreements of Bilaterals I and II are based on the notion of equivalence of laws between the two parties, and implementation and application of the agreements are based on mutual recognition of the relevant legislation. These agreements include consultation procedures in the event of changes to laws or regulations on either side, and explicitly set out how to adapt the agreements to legislative or regulatory changes if that is required. Typically the joint committee is authorised to make 'technical' changes to specified annexes and protocols of the agreements, but not to change the main provisions of any of the agreements as such.

Thus, the relevant joint committees can make changes to the annex of the *air transport* agreement, to eight of the ten annexes of the *land transport* agreement, to all of the annexes of the *public procurement* agreement, to both of the annexes of the agreement on *technical barriers to trade,* to annexes 1 and 2, as well as to the appendices of the other 9 annexes of the *agriculture* agreement, to annexes II and III (but not annex I) of the agreement on *free movement of persons,* to the two annexes of the *statistics* agreement, to the annexes of the environment agreement and to the annex of the agreement on Swiss participation in the *MEDIA* programme.

The Switzerland/Communities *Research* Committee and the joint committee in the agreement on the *fight against fraud* are on the other hand not authorised to make any changes to the respective agreements and their annexes. Likewise, the *Schengen* and *Dublin* Mixed Committees are not authorised to make any decisions concerning new legislation, as the adoption of new Schengen *acquis* is reserved to the EU institutions.

According to the Swiss Federal government, none of the agreements fulfilled the criteria for a compulsory referendum, which would have been necessary in case any of the agreements entailed the inclusion in a supranational organisation. However, reflecting the fact that most of the agreements are based on the equivalence of law, the entire Bilateral I was submitted to optional referenda. As noted in Chapter 2, the Swiss federal government and Parliament agreed that all nine contractual agreements of Bilateral II, except the agreement on processed agricultural products, would be submitted to an optional referendum. In the end, however, only the Schengen and Dublin association agreements received enough signatures for such a referendum to take place in June 2005.

In some agreements, Switzerland is explicitly committed to adopt the *acquis* in delineated areas and sectors. In the Dublin agreement, Switzerland commits itself to adopt the Dublin and Eurodac regulations governing asylum cooperation in the EU (Art. 1). If Switzerland is unable to except these changes, the agreement is suspended (Art. 4). On air transport, Switzerland has agreed to accept the *acquis* in the civil aviation sector (and that application and interpretation of the *acquis* is under the control of the EU institutions in specified areas). On the free movement of persons, the parties agreed to adopt measures enabling them to implement rights and obligations between them equivalent to those contained in the parts of the *acquis* to which the agreement refers. According to the land transport agreement, Switzerland agrees to apply regulations that are equivalent to those in the EU concerning access to the professions, social welfare, technical standards and weight limits. The statistics agreement envisages that EU acts of law on statistics become compulsory for Switzerland. Participation in the MEDIA programme is conditional on having legislation in the audio-visual sector that is EU-compatible, including the directive on Television without Frontiers. As Switzerland is already part of the Council of Europe's Convention on Transfrontier Television, there were few differences in this field, although Switzerland had to adapt its position on the film industry in the WTO to enable participation in MEDIA. The Joint Committee managing the environment agreement has the authority to make decisions with respect to accepting new EU law into the agreement related to the activities of the European Environmental Agency. Switzerland also had to adapt is laws concerning the buying and owning of firearms, on which the Schengen agreement sets minimum requirements. However, Swiss law already conformed largely to EU directives, and only minor changes to Swiss legislation are required. In the agreement on technical barriers to trade, the parties can agree to let already harmonised legislation be covered by the agreement.

Only one of the agreements of Bilateral II, the Schengen association agreement, could be regarded as a partial integration agreement, although this could be disputed depending on the choice of definition of the concept of 'partial integration'. Formally, the incorporation of new Schengen *acquis* into the EU-Swiss Schengen association agreement requires approval from the Swiss legislature every time. However, if Switzerland is unable to adopt new Schengen *acquis*, the agreement could eventually, in accordance with the procedures set out in Art. 7 of the Schengen association agreement, be terminated. This of course dramatically raises the cost of rejecting individual pieces of new Schengen *acquis* by Switzerland to the point of making it highly unlikely that Switzerland will exercise this right. In practice, therefore, the Schengen association agreement implies a general commitment by Switzerland to adopt EU rules and regulations in this policy area.

It should also be mentioned in this context that some of the agreements also allow for safeguard measures to be introduced under specific conditions. For instance, the agreement on the free movement of people will allow for the unilateral reintroduction of quotas in the case of a large influx of EU workers – defined as more than 10% of the average of the three preceding years – for two years during June 2007- June 2014 period. The land transport agreement contains a 'consensus-based' safeguard clause in case of serious disturbances to the flow of traffic.

3.6   The settlement of disputes

In all but one of the agreements of Bilaterals I and II, any conflicts between the parties are to be settled by the bilateral committees, in accordance with the mechanisms and procedures of international law. Disputes between the contractual parties can neither be submitted to the European Court of Justice nor to the Swiss courts. The absence of any legal remedies against decisions of the bilateral committees and the fact that there is no surveillance authority to monitor compliance, combined with the dynamic development of (some of) the bilateral agreements, raise some important questions concerning the settlement of any disputes between the parties in the bilateral sectoral agreements.

The exception to the general rule of dispute settlement between the EU and Switzerland is the air transport agreement, where the EU institutions – the European Commission and the European Court of Justice – are given competences on competition in this field, including surveillance and dispute settlement (Arts 17-20). The usual dispute settlement procedure of the joint committees is inapplicable here, although all other matters covered by the air transport agreement are to be settled by the Joint Committee (Art. 29).

4. The bilateral sectoral approach in practice

4.1 The implementation of the bilateral agreements

4.1.1 From entry into force to full implementation

Before embarking on an assessment of the bilateral sectoral agreement, it should be noted that although Bilateral I entered into force in June 2002 (and three of the agreements of Bilateral II – the agreements on processed agricultural products, taxation of savings and pensions – entered into force in 2005), few of the agreements of Bilateral I were fully implemented on 1 June 2002. Indeed, it will take almost another decade before all seven agreements in Bilateral I and all nine agreements of Bilateral II are fully implemented.

4.1.1.1. Postponed implementation. The somewhat later than expected end of negotiations and entry into force of Bilateral I had consequences for several of the agreements, in particular those envisaging the participation of Switzerland in the EU's multi-year programmes. When the research agreement was negotiated, the aim was for Switzerland to participate in the 5th Framework Programme (1998-2002), which expired at the end of 2002. According to the agreement, the financial provisions would take effect on 1 January the year after entry into force. Since Bilateral I did not enter into force until 1 June 2002, the agreement did not take full effect. However, another provision provided for the possibility of renewal to allow full Swiss participation in the 2002-06 6th Framework Programme (FP6). The research agreement allowing for Swiss participation in the FP6 was renewed by the Commission in January 2003 and initialled by the two parties in September 2003. It was agreed to apply the agreement on a provisional basis from January 2004 onwards. Switzerland thus continued its previous participation on a project-by-project basis for more than a year and a half after the entry into force of the research agreement.

A similar development is occurring concerning Swiss participation in EU programmes envisaged in agreements in Bilateral II. For legal reasons, it was not possible for Switzerland to participate in current EU programmes on education, training and youth as envisaged in the agreement. The European Commission made a unilateral declaration in June 2002, stating that it would propose the possibility of Swiss participation in the next generation of programmes from 2007 onwards to the Council and the European Parliament.

4.1.1.2. Transition periods. A second and more significant reason why the entry into force did not entail full implementation of Bilateral I in June 2002 is that most of the bilateral agreements allow for significant transition periods for certain provisions. As a consequence, it will not be possible to assess the full impact of the agreements for several years to come.

The most significant example of transition periods are in the agreement on the free movement of persons. The rights and obligations under the free movement agreement are phased in through several stages. In the first stage, which lasted for two years after entry into force, i.e. until June 2004, the two parties were allowed to continue to give priority to own nationals in employment, and the country's own laws on employment terms and conditions continued to be applied. This did not, however, apply to EU nationals already living and working in Switzerland and Swiss nationals already living and working in the EU, and priority for nationals in favour of these people was not allowed. During the first five years, i.e. until June 2007, Switzerland is able to limit the number of short-term work permits to no less than 115,000 and long-term permits to no less than 15,000. On social security, vested benefits cannot be received in cash after a five-year period following entry into force, unless the person leaving Switzerland does not join a similar scheme in the EU. Full freedom of movement between the EU and Switzerland will only be introduced in June 2014, 12 years after the entry into force of the agreement. The protocol extending the agreement on free movement of persons after the 2004 enlargement sets out the specific quotas, as well as longer transition periods for the new members.[28]

The commercial flying rights granted to Swiss airlines in the EU under the air transport agreement are phased in gradually. Most of the so-called 'eight freedoms of civil aviation' were granted at the date of entry into force of the agreement in June 2002, such as overfly rights and the right to non-commercial stopovers, as well as access to the important route between Zürich and Paris. Grand cabotage was allowed by the agreement from June 2004 (Art. 15 (1)), two years after its entry into force, while negotiations on the eighth freedom, cabotage, are to commence in 2007, five years after the entry into force of the agreement (Art. 15 (3)).

In the agreement on land transport, the prices charged by Switzerland for traffic through Switzerland by heavy goods vehicles, the so-called HGV tax, as well as the weight limits for such trucks, will be phased in gradually. The weight limit remained at 28 tonnes until 2001, was then increased to 34 tonnes until 2005, when the 40 tonne limit envisaged in the agreement was introduced. During the transition period until 2005, the EU received annual quotas for vehicles above the size limit. The HGV tax will increase drastically, from 40 CHF (approximately €25) until 2001 to 172 CHF in the 2001-05 period, to 293 CHF between 2005 and 2008, and 325 CHF (approximately €210) thereafter. Grand cabotage limits are removed in 2005.

Further, the withholding tax introduced in Switzerland as a result of the agreement on taxation of savings will be phased until 2011. The tax rate, currently set at 15%, will rise to 20% between July 2008 and July 2011, and finally to 35% from July 2011. The removal of tariffs on cheese, considered by the Swiss Integration Bureau to be the 'cornerstone' of the agriculture agreement, will apply from June 2007, five years after the entry into force of the agreement.

Switzerland negotiated two special provisions in the Schengen association agreement related to the matter of transition periods. The adoption of new *acquis* is not automatic under the Schengen association agreement, but must be approved each time by the Swiss legislature. In light of the relatively lengthy Swiss legislative process, the agreement

---

[28] See Lasowski (2005, p. 25) for an overview of the transition periods.

grants a two-year period for new Schengen *acquis* to pass through the Swiss legislative process. Secondly, Switzerland obtained what the Swiss Integration Bureau describes as a 'perpetual exception' in the event that Schengen cooperation develops to give rise to an obligation for legal assistance with regard to evasion of direct taxation. This was done in order to protect Swiss banking secrecy. Switzerland has further been guaranteed the 'principle of speciality' which ensures that the exchange of information on judicial assistance is not used in cases relating to direct taxation.

4.1.1.3. Validity of agreements. Most of the bilateral agreements between the EU and Switzerland are concluded for a definite period. Typically they will be automatically extended indefinitely unless one of the parties chooses to withdraw from the agreement, although there are different possibilities and mechanisms for extension and/ or revision and/or renewal in each of the agreements. The agreement on the free movement of persons is initially valid for a seven-year period, i.e. until 1 June 2009, and is automatically renewed for an indefinite period unless either party notifies a decision to the contrary before the expiry of the agreement. The continuation of the agreement is to be confirmed by a referendum in Switzerland. A possible revision of the savings tax agreement will be jointly undertaken in 2013. In other cases, the duration of the agreement depends on the duration of various EU multi-annual programmes, for instance on research and in the audio-visual sector. The participation of Switzerland in FP6 and MEDIA is terminated when these programmes end their life-cycles in 2006. Swiss participation in the respective successor programmes will then be the subject of new negotiations.

4.1.2 Incorporation of new acquis

4.1.2.1. The development of new acquis. The EU has launched a number of broader policy initiatives in many of the areas covered by Bilateral I since the agreements were signed in 1999. Most of these initiatives envisage legislative measures, some of which have already been introduced.

There have for instance been considerable changes in the field of air transport. In the aftermath of the September 11, 2001 terrorist attacks in the US, the EU has adopted a raft of legislation on air safety and security. Secondly, the 'Single European Sky' initiative launched in 1999 was adopted in 2004, consisting of four new regulations. In the area of overland transport, the EU is in the midst of adopting three packages liberalising the railway sector in Europe. The directives of the first package entered into force in 2003, while the measures of the second package are currently being discussed in the EU institutions. The Commission unveiled its proposals for the third package in 2004. The idea of creating a 'European Research Area' was launched at the March 2000 European Council as part of the so-called 'Lisbon agenda' to make the EU the most competitive economy in the world by 2010.

Beyond these broader new initiatives, the EU continues to adopt and update existing *acquis*. On the free movement of people, EU legislation was consolidated in 2004. Two regulations and nine directives were repealed and replaced with a new directive. Public procurement legislation, previously contained in four directives, was similarly updated and consolidated in two directives adopted in 2004.

One of the principal tasks of the Swiss Mission to the EU in Brussels is to gather information on legislative developments in the EU. The Federal Offices with their experts and task groups then examines the compatibility of new legislation with the agreements. Their conclusions are either that the new piece of legislation does not have any effect on the specific agreement, that it affects the agreement but that existing legislation is compatible with the legislative change, or that the new legislation requires adaptation of the specific agreement in question. Usually these entail minor technical changes to the annexes of the agreements. In several of the agreements, the joint committee has the competence to make such adaptations of the agreements.

Since, in theory, Switzerland is not bound by rulings of the European Court of Justice (ECJ) taken after the date of 21 June 2001, Switzerland shall be informed if the ECJ changes its practice in a case touching the area of a specific agreement. The relevant joint committee will then discuss the effects of the new practice and can make a decision on the analogue application of the new ruling.

4.1.2.2. Decision-shaping. Switzerland plays a negligible role in the development of the *acquis*. The bilateral agreements allow for a limited participation by Swiss experts in the committees preparing legislation for the Commission. The Commission is committed to consult with Swiss experts on an equal basis with experts from EU member states in fields where Swiss legislation is recognised as equivalent to the *acquis*. In connection with the conclusion of the Bilateral I package, the EU Council of Ministers adopted a declaration granting Swiss representatives the right to participate as 'active observers', with a right to speak, but not to vote, in committee meetings in the areas of research, air transport, social security and recognition of diplomas. Although decision-shaping is not meant to be a function of the bilateral committees, very often the Swiss representatives in the committees are also sent to participate on behalf of Switzerland in the European Commission committees preparing legislation where Switzerland is granted access.

Beyond the 'pre-pipeline' stage of legislative preparation, Swiss representatives are not present. Not surprisingly in this context, the provision of adequate and timely information emerged as another important issue in the interviews. On the matter of transparency, there were notable differences among the European and Swiss officials interviewed for this study. Among the Swiss interlocutors, a minority was quite satisfied, characterising the information flow as easy and informal (by e-mail or telephone) throughout the whole year. A majority, however, thought that Switzerland is disadvantaged because of its position as a non-member country. According to this group, first of all, Switzerland is dependent on good sources in the EU to get the information needed concerning actions in the EU. The flow of information is judged to be inadequate because Switzerland very often has to get the information itself (especially in cases when the Swiss EU Mission in Brussels is not deeply involved). In the same context, it was often mentioned that the information flow is even deficient within Switzerland itself and needs to be improved. The information deficit seems less of a problem in the more dynamic agreements, which provide, perhaps not surprisingly, for the most extensive cooperation and participation in EU structures. However, in the case of the Schengen agreement, this does not include the crucial first step of consultations when it is decided whether a new JHA measure is 'Schengen-relevant' and should therefore be incorporated into the Schengen association agreements, or whether it falls outside the scope of the Schengen agreement. In the latter case, the participation of non-EU member states requires a separate agreement.

Lack of information was not considered a problem on the EU side, and the topic was not raised in most of the interviews. When it did come up, EU officials expressed the view that Switzerland managed quite well to keep itself informed about EU developments in general and about relevant new EU laws in particular. This was to a large extent due to the drawn-out legislative process within the EU, which gives the Swiss side ample time to familiarise itself with new EU laws and regulations, but also a result of consultations through the joint committee system.

4.1.2.3. Decision-making in the bilateral committees. The bilateral committees are typically authorised to make 'technical' changes, i.e. adaptations to (some of) the annexes of the agreements, which mainly consist of lists of references to the *acquis*. Although the rules of procedure of each agreement typically stipulate that the chair of the joint committees rotates between the EU and Switzerland, and that it is the responsibility of the chair to set the agenda, according to EU officials it is in practice the EU that takes the initiative to have new *acquis* incorporated into the agreements.

On the Swiss side, decisions falling within the competence of the joint committee only require the approval of the Federal Council. In case the decision would need an adaptation of Swiss statute law, the joint committee can only make its final decision if the statute law adaptation is first approved by the Federal Assembly and, in case a referendum is also required in Switzerland, by the people.

The decision-making process. Once it is concluded that an agreement needs to be amended to take legislative changes in the EU into account, the parties have to examine whether and in what form the new legislation shall be integrated into the agreements. This process can be quite fast, if the new regulation simply replaces an outdated regulation in the annex. In other cases, however, the process is more complicated.

When Switzerland does not wish to integrate a new piece of legislation into the agreement, the EU has to decide whether it agrees with the proposed Swiss derogations or not. The proposition will circulate between the parties as long as they don't fully agree. These procedures slow down the already complicated decision process further, as the Federal Offices and the European Commission require the approval by their respective governments.

Following a decision to incorporate new legislation into any of the agreements, the Federal Justice Office and the Directorate for International Law of the Foreign Affairs Office examines whether the Federal Assembly needs to be consulted. Eventually the cantons will have to be consulted and/or the Federal Assembly (Presidents of the Chambers, Foreign Policy Commission). The Swiss Integration Bureau and the head of the Swiss delegation to the relevant bilateral committee are in charge of coordinating these actions.

The decision is prepared by the rotating chair of the joint committee. When Switzerland holds the chair, the draft text is prepared by experts in the relevant Federal Office in collaboration with the Swiss EU Mission in Brussels and the Integration Bureau, often in consultations with various interest groups. The draft is then legally examined by the Federal Office of Justice and/or the Directorate of International Law in the Foreign Affairs Office, before the Federal Council decides on the adoption of the proposal and commissions the negotiation mandate. The delegations in the joint committee will hereafter inform each other and negotiate and compare the proposal for adoption. If the joint committee does not agree, the proposal will again be revised following the consultation procedures described above.

Once agreement on a text is reached in the bilateral committee, it is submitted to the respective authorities of each party, on the Swiss side by the Federal Office in charge of the dossier to the Federal Council, for formal approval. The leaders of the delegations to the joint committee can then sign the document. In case there is no request for an optional referendum and the approval of the Federal Assembly is not needed, the adaptation decision of the joint committee enters into force upon publication in the Bundesblatt (BBl.) and usually, in the form of notification, in the Amtliche Sammlung des Bundesrechts (AS).

Many of the officials interviewed complained that the decision-making process in the bilateral committees was a very slow and unwieldy process, due in part to the elaborate examination of legislative compatibility undertaken by Switzerland as well as the consultation mechanisms, where speedy agreement is hindered by the relatively infrequent meetings of the bilateral committees. The process of transposition of new EU *acquis* in the 'dynamic' agreements such as the air and overland transport agreements is judged to be particularly slow and unwieldy by Swiss officials involved. Once a decision on implementation has been made, the speed of procedure depends on one hand on the complicated legislation procedure in Switzerland, but also on the complicated mechanisms in the EU. The whole procedure can take up to 1 – 1½ years until the new EU *acquis* can enter into force in Switzerland. This has however created only a few minor problems that were either ignored or resolved at a lower level and have so far not led to any political disputes between the EU and Switzerland. This systemic challenge remains and could be more likely to result in difficulties once all of the agreements are fully implemented.

Experiences on incorporation of new acquis. A law commonly known as Eurolex, drawn up before the EEA referendum in December 1992, introduced the requirement that all new Swiss legislation should be compatible with EU legislation. In spite of the 'no' vote on the EEA, this law has continued to be applied, and it was estimated that as much as 85% of new Swiss legislation was EU-compatible by the late 1990s.[29] The fact that all new Swiss legislation had been made compatible with that of the EU for almost a decade when Bilateral I entered into force in 2002 lessened its direct and immediate impact and reduced the need for legislative changes in Switzerland in order to implement Bilaterals I and II. The agreement on technical barriers to trade is one example, which had a limited impact on Swiss regulations and standards as such, as Swiss standards to a large extent already conformed to EU standards, in compliance with the Swiss law on technical barriers to trade adopted in October 1995. On Schengen, Switzerland has already switched towards a greater use of mobile controls, with only sporadic controls at the border. Swiss participation in major international organisations and treaties, such as the UN, the Council of Europe and the WTO, entails a significant amount of alignment and harmonisation of national policies and laws of participating states, and has further facilitated the implementation of the bilateral agreements with the EU.

Up until today there has not been the need for substantial changes to Swiss statute law.[30] Art. 7a RVOG[31] entails that the Federal Council (and the delegated mandate to the joint committee) would not be competent to adopt the treaty alone, but needed the approval by the Swiss parliament. The EU-Swiss joint committee would have to wait for the assent of the Federal Assembly before making the decision on adaptation of the

---

[29] Sverdrup & Kux (1997, pp. 10-11).

[30] The introduction of the European Air Safety Agency (EASA) into the agreement on air transport provoked an adaptation of Art. 3 of the Swiss Statute of Air Transport (LFG), to which the Federal Assembly had to agree, in addition to the approval of the introduction of the EASA regulation. This single adaptation cannot be considered to be substantial.

[31] See Chapter 2.5.2.

agreement. The presumption concerning substantial developments in EU law affecting Switzerland is that Switzerland has in the end no choice but to adopt the new *acquis*, if only for economic reasons. A possible rejection by the Federal Parliament of a change of Swiss statute law to adapt to new *acquis* would broaden the gap between EU law and 'Swiss *acquis*' and could endanger the existence of the bilateral agreements as such.

Among the agreements of Bilateral I, the air transport agreement goes furthest in terms of integration between the EU and Switzerland. In addition to the new civil aviation legislation on air safety and security and on the 'single European sky', the joint committee also had to contend with a backlog of legislation adopted in the EU between the signing of Bilateral I and its entry into force two-and-a-half years later. The Joint Committee has met four times since the entry into force of the agreement in June 2002. In addition, the two parties meet at expert level once or twice per year to prepare the meetings of the Joint Committee. The Joint Committee made three decisions on amending the annexes of the agreement in 2004 and one in 2005, with at least three expected for 2006, including one on Swiss participation in the European Air Safety Agency (EASA).

The dynamic development in EU civil aviation policy has created some amount of friction in EU-Swiss relations, Switzerland was for instance initially reluctant to accept the inclusion of references to new (or revised) legislation on ground-handling and night-boarding into the annex of the air transport agreement, arguing that these were not necessary for the good functioning of the agreement. Due to these disagreements, implementation of the night-boarding directive in Switzerland did not take place as originally envisaged in 2004. A long list of directives and regulations has recently been agreed upon, and will be incorporated into the agreement in early 2006, including the directive on night-boarding.

In spite of these minor problems, it is also noteworthy that the negotiations on security-related legislation on air transport were brief and did not trigger any demands for any derogations beyond minor technical adaptations. It should further be noted that the two parties agreed not to use the air transport Joint Committee as the venue for the dispute over the Zürich airport (see below).

A few problems have also emerged concerning the overland transport agreement, mainly related to implementation issues. Switzerland here typically chooses to wait on EU member states with similar organisation of public services (for instance, Germany and the

Netherlands). There have also been some minor issues raised in the agreement on technical barriers to trade concerning chemicals, while the proposed reduction of EU sugar subsidies could cause some problems for the agreement of processed agricultural products. There have also been certain problems concerning earlier agreements, for instance concerning the radioactivity warning systems, an area in which the EU is currently revising its legislation.

Another problem encountered in several cases concerns the difficulties and differences in defining the precise boundaries of the various agreements. One aspect of this is the role and relevance of EU case law and specific rulings of the European Court of Justice. There have been a number of such cases in the bilateral agreements, for example concerning air transport and the free movement of persons. The consolidation of the *acquis* on free movement of persons was accompanied by changes in the jurisprudence of the European Court of Justice, which the Joint Committee has agreed to take into account. Questions have also been raised concerning the reach of the provision on services in this agreement. A specific case related to the principle of equal treatment in the agreement on free movement of persons was raised by Switzerland, which argued that differentiated entrance fees between EU and Swiss citizens at certain museums and historical sites in Italy and Spain were against the agreement, basing its argument on specific ECJ rulings. According to the Commission, this ECJ case law was not relevant to the agreement, as it was adopted after the signing of Bilateral I. The Commission further replied that such an interpretation of the agreement would also extend to cover differentiated pricing of ski-passes in certain Swiss resorts. No decision on this issue has been made by the Joint Committee.

A second related issue has emerged where the sectoral agreements do not cover the entire area of cooperation in the EU in that policy domain, such as the Schengen agreement and EU cooperation in the field of justice and home affairs. The determination as to whether new justice and home affairs *acquis* is 'Schengen-relevant' becomes a key question. The applicability of ECJ rulings has emerged as an issue of contention also in the case of the Zürich airport and the air transport agreement (see below).

All of these are examples of relatively few and quite minor issues of contention, and as a rule, the two sides find agreement on adjusting the bilateral agreements to the development of new *acquis*. There have been a few Swiss attempts to diverge from EU legislation, but apart from areas of key Swiss national interest and where Switzerland has some political leverage, for instance on overland transport and in banking, these efforts have according to Swiss officials not been successful. Such an attempt to depart from EU legislation in the field of air transport was indeed met by a series of *démarches* from the EU to Switzerland, criticising the latter for their interpretation of the agreement and warning against attempts at 'cherry-picking' the *acquis*.

Taking into account that Bilateral I has been in force for less than three years, a pattern seems to emerge concerning the discussions between the EU and Switzerland on the incorporation of new *acquis* into the bilateral agreement. While the latter attempts a more restricted line, arguing that new EU legislation is not directly relevant to a specific bilateral agreement, the EU argues for a broader interpretation. Many Swiss officials noted that Switzerland usually is in the weaker position relative to the EU in case it expresses reservations concerning a regulation to be implemented. The EU normally takes notice of a Swiss reservation, but often takes no action, and the ensuing situation of non-compatible legislation is allowed to persist. Ultimately, however, Switzerland typically feels compelled by its interest in market access and the benefits of equivalence of law to implement the EU regulation. Indeed, all EU officials, as well as most Swiss officials, agree that even in areas where Switzerland is not formally bound to implement the *acquis*, such as in the so-called 'static agreements', the economic benefits of compatible legislation is such that Switzerland does so in the end.

There are several reasons why this pattern has emerged. The first, and most obvious, explanation is that it simply reflects the balance of power and interests between the EU and Switzerland. Access to EU markets or participation and association with EU policies, programmes and agencies are far more important to Switzerland than access to Swiss markets and Swiss participation in EU activities are to the EU.

Secondly, the EU has recently changed its policy on temporary exceptions and permanent derogations in relations with third countries. While permanent exemptions were not unheard of before then, the EU now has a policy of not accepting such derogations. This change in policy was a direct result of the 2004 enlargement process. The EU received a very large number of detailed requests for permanent derogations from the candidate states in the early 2000s, and decided in 2002 on a more restrictive line in relations with third countries on the issue of exemptions, in general not accepting any permanent derogations. The enlarged EU is an increasingly heterogeneous Union, which makes it more difficult for the EU to be flexible and accept special derogations vis-à-vis non-member states.

This shift in general EU policy is compounded by the perception among EU officials that the relationship with Switzerland is unnecessarily complicated. The management of the numerous bilateral sectoral agreements requires considerable time and resources on the EU side, which many EU officials find unwarranted in light of the overall significance of Switzerland to the Union. EU officials noted that senior officials and political leaders in the EU often found it difficult to find common ground with their Swiss counterparts, as the latter seemed to give far greater attention to the details and specificities of the various agreements, rather than taking a more 'political' view of the relationship.

This seems related to the general perception among EU officials that Switzerland was the *demandeur* for the current (complex) state of the relationship, and thus ultimately responsible for its functioning. While the relationship is considered to be good and the bilateral agreements functioning well, EU officials seemed in agreement that it would be up to Switzerland to find workable solutions to any possible problems that may arise. Swiss officials, on the other hand, emphasised that a number of the bilateral sectoral agreements, for instance on savings tax and a possible agreement on energy transit, had been formally requested by the EU side. It was also noted that the bilateral approach with Switzerland causes difficulties in relations with other third countries, notably with and among other EFTA countries, and that from a management perspective, it would be much easier for the EU if Switzerland was part of the EEA.

Finally, Swiss agreement on the EU's interpretation is also a result of the 'appropriate parallelism' which the EU insisted upon in the negotiations of Bilateral I. There are political and legal linkages between the agreements that reduce the de facto autonomy of Switzerland. First there is the so-called 'guillotine clause' in Bilateral I. While there is no such general linkage in Bilateral II, there is a 'mini-guillotine' linking Schengen and Dublin and the agreements with the other associates in this area (Norway and Iceland). There are also other linkages between the agreements that are not legal and thus contested, notably the link between Schengen and the agreement of free movement of persons. All EU officials interviewed concurred with the opinion expressed by Commissioner Benita Ferrero-Waldner that it is not possible to have a Schengen association without an agreement on free movement of persons. The absence of a legal requirement is here related to the opt-outs of certain member states from Schengen cooperation. These linkages raise the potential cost of rejecting individual pieces of legislation.

4.1.3   Dispute settlement in practice

There have been no significant disputes between the EU and Switzerland concerning any of the agreements of Bilateral I since they entered into force three and a half years ago. The Swiss approach to the question of dispute settlement could be described as pragmatic. According to the Swiss interlocutors, it has so far not been necessary to resort to the formal arbitration process in the joint committees as set out in the bilateral agreements. If the parties did not agree on a specific question, this was discussed in a friendly manner. If a solution was not found, the matter would be postponed to a further meeting and it was declared that the parties promise to examine the question under dispute.

However, although most of the officials interviewed were rather relaxed concerning the use of dispute settlement in the joint committees, some of the interlocutors voiced a general concern about the design of the formal dispute settlement mechanism. This essentially entails that a dispute should be settled in the joint committees among the same individuals that were unable to reach agreement in the first place.

The case of the Zürich airport (see Box 4) currently pending before the European Court of Justice provides another example of disagreement related to the Court and the relevance of its rulings on the bilateral agreements. The case is indeed unique in the history of the EU, as it is the first time a non-member state has brought the European Commission before the Court. Even though this is not explicitly provided for in the agreement, the case was accepted and was referred to the Court of First Instances in accordance with normal internal EU procedures. An eventual ECJ decision in favour of the position of Germany and the Commission could lead to a considerable reduction in traffic at Zürich airport, which again could have implications for Zürich as an international commercial and financial centre.

Box 4. The Zürich airport case (Case C-70/04)

On 16 February 2004, the Swiss Confederation brought an action against the European Commission to the European Court of Justice to annul a decision relating to the use of German airspace by aircraft approaching and departing from the Zürich airport.

This use of German airspace was governed by a bilateral agreement between Switzerland and Germany until the latter terminated the agreement with effect from 31 May 2001. A new agreement was negotiated and subsequently signed, but it has not been ratified by either party.

Germany published a new regulation (No. 213) for the implementation of German air traffic regulations in January 2003, which was subsequently amended in April 2003. Regulation 213 sets a number of limitations for the approach to Zürich airport, including minimum waiting levels, specific sets of landing procedures, and imposing the use of five routes for planes taking off from Zürich airport.

In June 2003, the Swiss government requested that the Commission make a decision to the effect that Germany could not continue to apply regulation 213. This was followed by an interim agreement between Switzerland and Germany whereby the latter agreed to suspend application of the regulation for a few months. However, Switzerland persisted in its complaint vis-à-vis the Commission.

Having received comments and further information from the two parties, the European Commission decided in Germany's favour on 5 December 2005. This was based in part on ECJ judgements (*Malpensa* and *Karlstad*) that the Swiss arguments fall outside the scope of the air transport agreement.

A ruling on the Zürich airport case is currently pending before the Court of First Instances of the European Communities.

Sources: Commission Decision of 5 December 2003, Official Journal L4/13, (2004/12/EC) 8.1.2004. Order of the Court (Second Chamber) of 14 July 2005, Official Journal C 296/8, (2005/ c295/15), 26.11.2005.

The question of dispute settlement did not arise in the interviews with EU officials, with the exception of the Zürich airport case. This was mainly because there have not been any disputes so far that required settlement, but also the perception shared by all EU officials interviewed that the solution would in any case, in the end, always be in accordance with EU policy and law. It was noted that possible problems, none of which has been very important so far, were discussed amicably in the bilateral committees.

The absence of disputes has several potential explanations. One would be to regard this as evidence that a functioning system has been established. Emerging issues and potential issues of disputes are often handled and resolved by desk officers in the Commission and the Swiss administration even before they reach the senior officials in the joint committees.

Another interpretation is that it is simply too early to tell. The agreements have as of early 2006 only been in force for about three and a half years, and have not so far required any change to Swiss statute law. Many of the key provisions in some of the more important agreements have not yet been implemented as they are subject to considerable transition periods, for instance on the introduction of free movement of people, which will only occur towards the middle of the next decade.

Another potential explanation for the absence of disputes is that there is a considerable commonality of interest between the EU and Switzerland, and that the bilateral agreements are in a fundamental sense 'win-win' situations. Finally, it could be claimed that one should in fact expect few disputes, as one of the basic 'rules' of EU association and cooperation agreements – that harmonisation is based on the *acquis* – is applicable also to EU-Swiss relations. While the agreements are not always presented in this manner to the Swiss public, its officials all seem to accept what the 'equivalence of law' entails in practice:

> When the EU concludes an agreement with any third country, it does not accept the establishment of harmonised regulations that might differ in any way from the *acquis communautaire*.[32]

4.1.4 *Transparency*

The issue of transparency was raised by most interlocutors. The complexity of the system in practice makes it difficult, even for officials directly involved in the process, to have a correct overview of the structure of the entire system (such as the number of agreements and bilateral committees)

---

[32] Fact sheet on Bilateral I of the Swiss Integration Bureau (downloaded from www.europa.admin.ch).

and the current state of play of the relationship. A number of specific problems relating to this theme were raised by the officials interviewed, in particular on the Swiss side.

4.1.4.1 Different aspects of transparency. Problems related to transparency emerged in discussions about many of the bilateral sectoral agreements. The agreements entail provisions for the joint committees to decide on their own rules of procedure. Those rules of procedure and the minutes of the meetings are usually not accessible to the public, as the joint committees are institutions of international law, which creates an obvious problem concerning the transparency of the bilateral agreements. Another aspect relates to the fact that the bilateral committees are managed by different administrative departments.[33] The decentralised nature of this system allows the various joint committees to 'live their own lives' to a greater extent than is typically the case in EU external relations. This was seen by some interlocutors as a growing problem. One issue raised by EU officials was that the various joint committees adopted different basic positions on the scope and relevance of EU legislation in the different bilateral agreements.

Another aspect of the transparency issue related to the implementation in Switzerland of already-adopted EU regulations and directives. The courts, attorneys-at-law and, of course, also officials in the federal or cantonal administration positions are confronted with a number of issues in different areas of law governed or linked to one of the bilateral agreements. It appears to be hard to know where to get the information needed and to search for the applicable provisions of law. Even Swiss officials found it difficult to obtain information about EU regulations adopted by Switzerland, especially in the dynamic (parts of) the agreements on issues such as social security or diplomas.

Yet another aspect of transparency raised in connection with the bilateral agreements concerns the openness of the Swiss government and administration towards the public. This issue was mainly voiced by Swiss interlocutors, and was not raised as a problem by the EU side. Some officials and experts interviewed claimed that the transparency of the 'true

---

[33] The agreement on free movement of persons is for instance managed by the Federal Migration Department, the air transport agreement is managed by the Federal Civil Aviation Department (BAZL), and so forth.

and technical effects' upon Switzerland and its legislation is restrained in the sense that the public is provided with only politically correct information. The development in Switzerland in recent years, however, shows that the need for more transparency has been acted upon.

4.1.4.2. Institutions and legal basis of transparency. In order to understand the importance attached to the topic of transparency in connection with the bilateral agreements between the EU and Switzerland and the acquis in Switzerland, it is useful to know which institutions are entrusted with the publication of laws and their communication to the public.

There are three different levels of institutions entrusted with the publication and communication with the general public in connection with treaties such as the bilateral agreements. At the highest political level, this is the responsibility of the Federal Chancellery. The Integration Bureau, as the leading agency on European affairs, plays the principal role in disseminating information to the public at the level of the federal administration. Thirdly, each federal office and department have responsibilities for communication and transparency in specific agreements, for instance the Federal Traffic Office in connection with the overland transport agreement, the Federal Migration Office in connection with the agreement on free movement of persons, etc.

The Federal Chancellery has a pivotal function between the government, the administration, the Federal Assembly and the public.[34] The Chancellery is responsible for the publication of the *corpus juris* of Switzerland: the Official Register of Federal Law (*Amtliche Sammlung* (AS)) and the Systematic Register of Federal Law (*Systematische Sammlung* (SR)). The legal basis for this – the Publication Statute and the connected Publication Ordinance – has recently undergone significant revision.[35] For the publication of international law texts, the statute now reduces the scope of compulsory publication, as treaties with limited importance do not

---

[34] Art. 1, Organisation Ordinance of the Federal Chancellery (Organistationsverordnung für die Bundeskanzlei (SR 172.210.10) of 5 May 1999.

[35] Bundesgesetz vom 18. Juni 2004 über die Sammlungen des Bundesrechts und das Bundesblatt, Publikationsgesetz, SR 170.512; AS 2004 4929; and Verordnung vom 17 November 2004 (SR 170.512.1; AS 2004 4937.

require publication in the AS.[36] In addition, decisions of international law that do not entail new legal binding provisions, such as most of the decisions of the joint committees, will only be announced in the form of a notification within the AS instead of being made public as the usual enacted legal provisions.[37]

Beyond the legal basis of publication, there is a significant trend towards a more open communication by Swiss authorities. The administration's actions have until today been explicitly governed by the principle of secrecy in Switzerland. The creation of a new statute for improved transparency of the administration was proposed in 2000, and a draft statute explicitly embracing the general principle of publicity, was endorsed by the Federal Assembly on 17 December 2004. A separate section on law enacted in connection with the bilateral agreements with the EU has furthermore been established on the homepage of the Swiss Confederation, and all of the texts of the agreements of Bilaterals I and II can be freely downloaded from the website of the Integration Bureau. The latter also includes a section on the decisions of the joint committees in each agreement, where the decisions on adaptation of the annexes are made public.[38]

4.1.4.3 Specific problems of transparency. The joint committees are accorded the power to adopt their own rules of procedure in the bilateral agreements, meaning that there are and will be as many sets of rules of procedure as there are joint committees. A few of these rules of procedure have been made public and are available on the Swiss government website. The rules of procedure of the Air Transport Joint Committee have for instance been made public, and those of the Schengen agreement – of which only a draft document has until now been available – is planned to be made public.

Since the joint committees are institutions of international law, the minutes of their meetings are as a general rule not made public. The meetings are usually followed by a press conference and a brief

---

[36] Art. 3, p. 3, Publication Statute, which entered into force on 1 January 2005.

[37] Art. 6 d, Publication Ordinance in connection with Art. 3 (1), c of the Publication Statute.

[38] See www.admin.ch(/ch/d/eur/index.html), and www.europa.admin.ch.

communiqué, however, which provides information on the main topics of the meeting.[39] While the communiqué lists the new *acquis* envisaged to be incorporated in the annexes of the agreements, it does not give any clues as to the positions of the two sides.[40] The Integration Bureau publishes a short note on meetings of the joint committees on its website after it has been debriefed on the meetings by the federal office or department in charge of the particular dossier in question. As soon as the minutes of the meetings have been approved by the EU and Swiss government, the decisions on the adaptation of the agreements are published on the homepage of the Swiss government and as a notification in the official journal (AS). According to officials interviewed, this last step of publication can take from a month up to one year.

The officials were asked for the reason of the policy of limited transparency. Most respondents answered that some of the issues and actions of the joint committees could appear politically sensitive and be misunderstood by the public. The reason for the limited transparency of the actions of the bilateral committees is of course their legal nature, being institutions of international law.

While improvements have been made, a lack of transparency vis-à-vis the Swiss public has further implications that should be taken into consideration. The question arises whether Switzerland is aware of the exact scope of the *acquis* and the consequent obligations which have been incorporated in Swiss legislation. And as a result of the reluctant and cautious communication policy of the Swiss government and administration both before and after the entry into force of the bilateral agreements, the Swiss public is left with the impression that the bilateral agreements are static, underestimating both the dynamic nature of (many of) the bilateral agreements, the continued evolution of EU rules and policies and their impact on how Switzerland is governed in practice.

---

[39] As an example, the main topics of this year's meeting on 5 July 2005 of the committee in the section of free movement of persons has been summarised in a communiqué issued by the Federal Migration Office (see www.bfm.admin.ch/user_upload/Aktuell/Pressemitteilungen).

[40] The communiqué of the Federal Traffic Office from 29 June 2005, for example, mentions that the first and the second package of EU directives on railway traffic have been discussed and could be incorporated at a later date.

4.2 The Europeanisation of Switzerland

4.2.1 Impact of the bilateral agreements on Switzerland

The bilateral sectoral agreements have required and resulted in significant changes to Switzerland in the last decade. Specific measures have been undertaken unilaterally in Switzerland to accommodate and facilitate the implementation of the bilateral agreements with the EU.

The most extensive such package has been the set of changes made to Swiss wage and labour policy to adapt to the agreement on the free movement of people, including significant changes in Swiss social welfare provisions.[41] The so-called 'accompanying measures' to the agreement on free movement of persons consisted of three main elements: a new law laying down minimum wages and working conditions for seconded employees working temporarily in Switzerland; ways of making it easier to declare collective labour agreements as binding; and standard employment contracts with minimum wages in areas without collective labour agreements. Tripartite commissions consisting of representatives of the authorities, the employers and the trade unions have been established at both federal and cantonal level to monitor the labour market and, if needed, to propose sanctions.

Although the agreement on free movement of persons entered into force in June 2002, the accompanying measures were only introduced in June 2004. The first experiences with the measures seem, however, to have been positive, and controls carried out in the second half of 2004 showed that the measures and the general wage and working conditions in Switzerland are adhered to. The Swiss experience with the agreement on free movement of persons has overall been positive. Total immigration to Switzerland has been slightly reduced since 2002 and the composition of immigrants have changed, with a growing share (and in absolute terms) of EU citizens residing in Switzerland. There has also been a slight increase in cross-border commuting since the agreement entered into force, largely offset by a decrease in the number of short-term residence permit holders.

The accompanying measures were strengthened in connection with the extension of the agreement of free movement of people to the new EU member states in Central and Eastern Europe. The measures included more

---

[41] Church (2000, pp. 13-14).

stringent sanctions in case of non-compliance with the law on secondment, a requirement that employers must notify the authorities in writing of its seconded workers in Switzerland, the appointment of labour market inspectors, measures to make it easier to declare collective labour agreements as binding, various measures against fictitious self-employment and better protection for temporary workers. An Accompanying Measures Task Force of federal and cantonal representatives and representatives of the social partners was established in 2004 to improve the implementation of the measures.

Numerous studies were commissioned by the Swiss government to assess the costs and benefits of the bilateral agreements, including specified costs and savings on the federal budget, as well as broader analyses of the impact the agreements would have on the Swiss economy and society. Studies commissioned in 1999 found that the Bilateral I package could increase the size of the Swiss economy by up to 2% in the long-term, or by approximately €5 billion. It has been estimated that the additional controls that are removed through the technical barriers to trade agreement represented approximately 0.5-1% of the total value of the products, in addition to delays caused by double-testing. On Bilateral II, it has been calculated that the extended scope of the agreement on processed agricultural goods would increase the volume of trade by one-third, worth almost €1 billion annually. The Dublin association agreement relieves some of the pressure on the Swiss asylum system. It has been estimated that 20% of all asylum applications in Switzerland are second applications. As an increasing number of European states are part of the Dublin Convention, Swiss non-participation could have increased the number of asylum applications in Switzerland.

Then there are the more diffuse benefits that are even more difficult to quantify. It is argued that having EU compatible statistics increases the attractiveness of Switzerland as a location for industry and also strengthens Switzerland in international negotiations. Further, access to EU film distribution structures draws more attention to Swiss films and brings a greater variety of European films to Switzerland. It is expected that the Swiss costs for its MEDIA participation will be more than compensated for by the benefits, including financial reimbursements, improved distribution and better marketing opportunities for Swiss films.

4.2.2   The bilateral agreements and the Swiss federal budget

The bilateral agreements have implications for the budget of the Swiss Federation. These include costs connected to participation in EU programmes as well as other contributions from Switzerland as a result of the bilateral agreements. Several of the agreements also have an impact on the expenditure and/or revenues of the Swiss federal government.

The Swiss government funds Swiss participation in the programmes on the basis of Gross Domestic Product (GDP), as do the EU member states. The total cost of this following the conclusion of Bilateral II will be approximately €100 million annually. The bulk of this contribution will be allocated to Swiss participation in the research framework programmes, much of which returns to Switzerland in the form of participation in projects by Swiss researchers. In the first calls for proposals under FP6, projects with Swiss participation had a higher success rate than the EU15 average.

In spring 2004, Switzerland agreed that it would make a financial contribution to the new EU member states of one billion Swiss francs (approximately €650 million) over the five-year period 2005-09.[42] The EU had requested such a contribution in 2003 following successful negotiations with the EFTA states in the EEA on raising the EEA financial contribution, which was increased five-fold, as well as a similarly-sized additional Norwegian contribution earmarked for the new member states. The rationale behind the EU's request was that the bilateral agreements provided Switzerland extensive access to the EU's internal market and that Switzerland should contribute to the costs of this single market, operationalised in the form of the EU's cohesion funds. The amount requested of Switzerland was based on the agreement on a financial contribution with the EFTA states negotiated in 2003. It was deemed reasonable that Switzerland would contribute one-third less than that provided by the other EFTA states, as the former did not have access to the single market in services due to the lack of an agreement on services. As of early 2006, negotiations on a Memorandum of Understanding on the Swiss financial contribution were almost concluded. The main outstanding issue was whether parts of the Swiss contribution should be allocated to 'old' EU

---

[42] *The Economist*, 22 May 2004.

member states such as Greece and Spain, or whether the entire sum should go to the new member states in Central and Eastern Europe.

The additional costs to the Swiss federal budget of the Bilateral I was estimated at about €400 million, while the impact of Bilateral II on the budget was much smaller. One-off costs related to the implementation of Bilateral I entail that current costs are slightly higher at around €500 million annually. The agreements with the most extensive additional costs in Bilateral I were the research agreement, overland transport (shifting traffic from road to rail), the agreement on free movement of persons (reduced sickness insurance premiums) and agriculture (loss of customs revenues). This includes the costs of participation in EU research programmes (approximately €70 million annually) and the co-financing of projects on overland transport. In some cases, these additional costs are not directly a result of the agreements. In the overland transport agreement, the principal additional costs are related to the shift of traffic from road to rail, a general goal of Swiss environmental policy.

Bilateral II also entails additional costs for the Swiss federal budget. Among the main items is a loss of approximately €50-60 million in loss of customs revenues as a result of the agreement on processed agricultural goods, and costs related to participation in the MEDIA programme, statistics, education, training and youth and the European Environmental Agency (in total approximately €25 million annually). Implementation of Dublin and Schengen also entails extra expenditure from the federal budget.

Some of the bilateral agreements also have positive effects on the Swiss federal budget. Based on the studies commissioned by the Swiss government on Bilateral I, it has been estimated that the tax revenues of the federal government could increase by as much as €700 million annually, and an even higher amount for the cantons, whose combined budgets are larger than that of the federal government, as a result of the expected 2% increase in GDP.

It has been estimated that the HGV tax introduced as part of the overland transport negotiations could bring in as much as €1 billion in revenues by 2007, a third of which comes from companies outside Switzerland. The two agricultural agreements will allow a reduction of subsides in Switzerland of almost €150 million per year. It has been estimated that Swiss participation in Dublin will reduce asylum costs by approximately €50 million per year. Switzerland will retain 25% of the revenues from the withholding tax introduced as a result of the agreement on taxation of savings, although it is difficult to estimate the revenue from this.

Overall then, and if these very approximate and uncertain estimates are broadly correct and a final agreement on the financial contribution is reached, the impact of the bilateral agreements will be roughly neutral as far as the Swiss federal budget is concerned. The cantons stand to gain considerably, mainly due to the higher tax revenues expected to emerge as a result of higher economic growth following the implementation of Bilaterals I and II, which is also a major contributing factor to the expected impact of the bilateral agreements on the Swiss federal budget. This does not, however, take account of the additional costs associated with the implementation of the bilateral agreements, which to a considerable extent falls on the cantons.

4.2.3   EU-Swiss relations and economic reforms in Switzerland

But the direct changes made in response to the bilateral agreements do not capture fully the impact of deepening European integration since the second half of the 1980s on Switzerland.[43] The prospect of Swiss participation in the EEA led directly to a number of significant changes to the Swiss political system in the early 1990s. Indeed, the expected participation in the EEA and its subsequent rejection by the Swiss people has probably had a greater impact on the Swiss political and constitutional system than changes introduced as a direct response to the bilateral agreements. Furthermore, these changes have arguably been more profound in the case of Switzerland than in many EU member states.

After the rejection of the EEA, the Swiss government launched an economic revitalisation programme in 1993 to improve the country's competitiveness.[44] This led to important reforms on competition policy and various sectoral reforms in such areas as telecommunications, agriculture, energy and transport. For instance, the Cartel Law was first reformed in 1995, the telecommunications sector in 1991 and 1997, and Swiss public procurement policies in 1994 and 1995, although the latter was primarily

---

[43] Mach et al. (2003).

[44] Ibid., p. 305.

due to the WTO agreement on public procurement markets as agreed under the Uruguay Round.[45]

The Domestic Market Act was adopted in 1998 to create a real single market in Switzerland in areas such as public procurement and professional services. Further changes to competition policy through a strengthening of anti-cartel legislation have recently been introduced through a new Cartel Law. Agricultural reforms introduced in the 1990s followed the policy shift within the EU, in which subsidies were directed away from price support towards direct support in order to minimise price distortion while maintaining income levels among Swiss farmers. One of the goals of agricultural reform was to reduce the price differences with the EU to half of the gap in 1998, but this has not been attained. Price support will be reduced further as a result of the Agriculture Policy 2007 initiative. Reform of the electricity markets, broadly following the EU's liberalisation approach, was undertaken in 2000, with an opening of the sector to competition phased in over a six-year period. In 2004, structural reforms were given a further boost through 17 policy measures to be introduced in the current legislative period (2003-07), including a revision of the Domestic Market Act, as well as further reforms to public procurement policies and the energy and transport sectors.

In many cases, the bilateral agreements are themselves an important part of the reform package in a given sector. The overland transport agreement was thus a key component of the railway reforms launched in 1999, as well as the 'Alps initiative' in the early 1990s. The introduction of VAT (replacing a turnover tax) in Switzerland was approved in a referendum in November 1993. In 2001, Switzerland introduced a HGV (Heavy Goods Vehicle) tax supported by 57% of the voters in a referendum in September 1998, to a large extent due to the agreement on overland transport with the EU.

4.2.4 *European integration and the Swiss political system*

4.2.4.1 *The development of the Swiss Constitution.* Switzerland became a federal state with the adoption of the Swiss Constitution by the people and the Cantons in 1848. As the Constitution provides the popular right to

---

[45] Ibid.

demand a partial revision of the Constitution, many single provisions were incorporated into the framework over the years. A total revision of the Constitution was debated from the mid-1960s, but it only became a reality in 1999 with the adoption of a new Constitution.

The new Swiss Constitution is basically a comprehensive updating of the original Constitution. After the many partial revisions, the new Constitution has been improved in clarity, structure and language. Unwritten constitutional law, such as case law of the Federal Court in the field of human rights, was introduced and dispensable provisions were removed. Moreover, there have been changes in the content that are connected to the relationship between the federation and the cantons and to the parliamentary rights.[46] In addition to comprehensively updating the Constitution, the 1999 revision was motivated by the recognition that Switzerland needed to respond to European integration in particular and to internationalisation more generally.

Change of paradigm and the effect on the shift within the national powers. The provisions of the new Swiss Constitution concerning foreign policy reflect a fundamental change of paradigm from the introverted Swiss Confederation in the 19th century to a modern and open constitutional state. Adapting the Swiss political system to the accelerating processes of international integration and globalisation was another driving motivation behind the constitutional revision process.

One aspect of the processes of globalisation and internationalisation is the growing prominence of legislation in the negotiation and conclusion of international treaties. This includes both agreements based on the principle of mutual recognition of law, and the creation of harmonised and common legal bases.[47] As a consequence, national legislative procedures are moved to an international level of contract formation and to the connected diplomatic and political procedures, causing a shift within the national powers from the legislative to the executive branch.

Relations between government and administration. Coordination between the government and the administration on a negotiation mandate has become unwieldy and difficult as a result of the growing complexity of

---

[46] Häfelin & Haller (2001, N 58 ff).

[47] Cottier & Germann (2001, §5 N 1 ff).

international treaties. As a result of the growth and complexity of the bilateral contractual relationship with the EU, in addition to the broader impact of European integration, the Union plays an increasingly prominent role in the work of the federal administration. Traditionally one federal department assumes the leading role in the negotiation of a specific treaty, and is also responsible for consultations with the other interested and involved departments and private interest groups. Since the 1960s, relations with the EU and its precursors have been led by the Integration Bureau and the two departments of economics and foreign affairs that it serves, rather than units within each ministry. With the bilateral agreements, other ministries in Switzerland are increasingly engaged in the development of Swiss relations with the EU. This is part of a broader trend whereby international agreements increasingly affect several policy fields and thus many governmental departments, the internal processes have become cumbersome. The structures and remedies in Swiss administrative law for improving and facilitating the process of foreign policy-making seem to be missing.[48]

Relationship between government and parliament. There is a certain tension between the constitutional principle of approval of treaties by the parliament and the extended power of the Federal Council to conclude treaties autonomously (see Chapter 2.3.2). With the prospect of Swiss participation in the EEA followed by accession to the EU, the participatory rights of the Federal Assembly were revised and introduced in the Federal Parliament Act in 1992.[49] This called for systematic consultations by the Federal Council with the Foreign Affairs Committee before adopting the Swiss position in the EU Council of Ministers on decisions that would be directly applicable to Swiss law (regulations) or entail amendment of existing Swiss legislation (directives).[50] In spite of these changes, the parliament nevertheless still plays a subordinate role in foreign relations.[51]

---

[48] Ibid., § 5 N 18.

[49] 1992: Revision of the "Geschäftsverkehrgesetz", abolished 1 December 2003 and integration of the provisions on the consultation of the Parliament in the Federal Parliament Act (SR 171.10)

[50] Swiss Euroadmin Integration Report (1999, abstract, pp. 9-10).

[51] Honegger (2004, pp. 7 f.).

The Federal Assembly has also sought to utilise its possibilities for a 'pre-emptive' influence on foreign policy and the conclusion of treaties through the use of parliamentary resolutions formulating objectives for the design of treaties.[52] These resolutions are binding in the sense that the government is obliged to justify all deviance from the formulated objectives. In the course of the 'Yes to Europe' initiative, the Federal Council even submitted a counterproposal and explained its intention of not wanting to steer Switzerland towards EU membership independently but would make the steering dependent on a decision of the parliament.[53]

Unlike in the EU member states, the Swiss Federal Assembly is a so-called 'militia type' of parliament consisting of non-professional members that have other occupations on the side. According to Art. 170 of the Constitution, the Assembly is entitled to evaluate the efficiency of measures taken by the federal authorities. In 1991, the Federal Assembly decided with broad support to establish a procedure for parliamentary control of the administration (PCA). The expressed reason for this decision was explicitly that the Swiss parliament does not have the resources or the time to properly undertake this task. Although the Federal Assembly today takes a reinforced position in foreign affairs and is consulted on a regular basis, the question arises whether a parliament consisting of part-time politicians without any support staff is able to meet the challenges of globalisation and European integration.

The Confederation and the Cantons. The old Swiss Constitutions of 1848 and 1874 provided extensive powers and autonomy to the cantons. These powers have slowly shifted to the federal level, as a process of centralisation gradually diminished cantonal autonomy. One of the aims of the 1999 revision of the Swiss Constitution was to compensate for these long-term developments, placing more emphasis on the principle of cooperation than on the principle of self-rule as expressed by the autonomy of the cantons.[54]

---

[52] The meeting of the Federal Council with the presidents of the governmental parties in the 'von Wattenwyl-Gespräche' is politically significant in order to assure the consent of the Assembly to all important foreign affairs negotiations.

[53] Cottier & Germann (2001, § 5, N 26).

[54] Fleiner et al. (2005, N 227 ff).

In foreign affairs, the Confederation has to take into consideration the powers of the cantons as well as the protection of their interests (Art. 54). The consultation of the cantons in foreign policy affairs is now provided in Art. 55 of the Constitution. While Art. 55 applies generally to international treaties, it is generally acknowledged that it is mainly relevant to European affairs (although it may also have some relevance to the proposed Swiss-US free trade agreement). The detailed provisions on information and consultation mechanisms have additionally been incorporated in the new Federal Participation Act of 1 July 2000.[55] The cantons participate in the preparation of decisions of foreign policy that concern their powers or their essential interests. The Confederation must therefore inform the cantons in a timely and full fashion, and consult with them. The position of the canton has particular weight when the treaty concerns their competences. The cantons are also entitled to participate in international negotiations whenever appropriate.

Inadequate information flows between the cantons and the federal government during the EEA negotiations provided impetus for the creation of the Conference of the Cantonal Governments (KdK[56]) in 1993. All 26 cantons have become members of the KdK.[57] The aim of the Conference is the coordination of decision-making procedures among the cantons in order to exercise their collective influence on the federal level.[58] The cantons have concluded a framework agreement on cooperation with the Confederation. According to the agreement, the information and consultation shall principally be conducted by the KdK. The vote of 18 cantons is sufficient to make a decision. The cantonal statements shall be given by the KdK in the name of all cantons.

The cantons in Switzerland are involved at the federal level by a cantonal representative in each joint committee, elected by KdK. A representative of the cantons has now been elected to the Federal Department of Justice, and the KdK is also present at the Swiss EU Mission

---

[55] SR 138.1.

[56] Konferenz der Kantonsregierungen (KdK). Hereafter the Conference of the Cantons.

[57] Rahmenordnung über die Arbeitsweise der KdK und der Direktorenkonferenzen bezüglich der Kooperation von Bund und Kantonen (www.kdk.ch).

[58] Fleiner et al. (2005, N 729).

to the EU in Brussels. In spite of these developments, the cantons themselves depend very much on information from the departments and the government, especially if they are responsible for implementation in the relevant policy area.

4.2.4.1   Direct democracy and bilateralism

The popular right to request optional referenda for treaties involving multilateral harmonisation of law, such as many of the EU-Swiss bilateral agreements, can potentially have an impact on the future stability of contractual relations between the EU and Switzerland. Two optional referenda relating to the bilateral agreements with the EU took place in 2005: in June to approve the agreements on Schengen and Dublin and in September to support the extension of the agreement on the freedom of movement to the new EU member states in Central and Eastern Europe. While the Swiss people voted in favour on both occasions, the referenda highlighted the tensions between Swiss direct democracy and the bilateral sectoral agreements with the EU.

The agreement on the free movement of persons was concluded as a so-called 'mixed agreement', i.e. the contracting parties of Switzerland are both the European Community as such and the member states of the EU. This is also the reason why the agreement on the free movement of persons could not directly be applicable to the new European member states. The extension of the EU needed a separate contractual basis. The extension protocol – which constitutes this legal basis – is an integral part of the agreement on the free movement of persons.[59]

All agreements in Bilateral I are legally linked to one another by the so-called 'guillotine clause', which calls for all agreements to enter into force simultaneously and the automatic termination of all other agreements in the event that one of the agreements is terminated.[60] According to the

---

[59] Arts 4 and 6 of the extension protocol.

[60] Similarly worded provisions to this effect are set out in Art. 25 in the agreement on free movement of persons, Art. 36 in the air transport agreements, Art. 58 in the overland transport agreement, Art. 17 in the agreement on agriculture, Art. 21 in the agreement on technical barriers to trade, Art. 18 in the public procurement agreement and Art. 14 in the agreement on research.

(identical) final provisions of the agreements of Bilateral I, if any, one party terminates a single agreement of Bilateral I, all seven cease to apply six months after receipt of notification of non-renewal. In case Switzerland had voted against the extension protocol, the EU would have considered terminating the agreement on grounds that it was unacceptable to treat the citizens of the 'old' and the 'new' member states in a different manner.

As the interviews took place before the vote in September 2005, the respondents were asked the question of what effect a rejection of the extension protocol would have on the bilateral agreements with the EU. On the one hand, most officials interviewed assumed that the EU would not have reacted so radically as to terminate the agreements, but would have required Switzerland to establish a procedure ensuring the equal treatment of citizens of the new European member states. In the absence of such Swiss remedies, however, it seemed clear on both sides that the EU would not have any major inhibitions about invoking the 'guillotine clause'.

4.2.4.2 Federalism and the bilateral approach

The consultation mechanisms for the cantons in foreign relations have been improved both on a constitutional and technical level. The cantons are represented in the joint committees of the agreements affecting the cantons' interests and implementation tasks directly, such as the agreements on free movement of persons, overland transport, air transport and public procurement. Inter-cantonal task groups have been established in the areas of social security, recognition of diplomas, public procurement, air transport and overland transport to support the representatives of the cantons in the preparative work for the meetings of the joint committees. After the meetings of the joint committees, the representative of the cantons will inform the head of foreign policy affairs in the KdK secretariat and the latter will give the information to the task groups or cantonal governments.

With cantonal representatives in the joint committees and a permanent representative of the KdK in Brussels, most officials interviewed conceded that the consultation procedures of the cantons can hardly be improved at the international level. Domestically, however, the bilateral agreements have made the handling of the system of federalism more difficult.

The situation of the cantons in foreign policy affairs is special insofar as they are directly affected by EU integration processes. They are confronted with the technical challenge of implementing treaties. It is therefore very important for the cantons to be fully informed of the legislation and judicial procedures in the EU of relevance to the bilateral agreements. The interviews revealed that there was a problem in the very early phases of new negotiations. Often the cantons were faced with a *fait accompli*, as exploratory talks between the Swiss government and the EU on cooperation in a new area, in which the cantons were not involved, is often transformed into *de facto* negotiations of a draft agreement. It was also mentioned that the Confederation occasionally had decided on its own without consulting the cantons or consulting them too late. The new consultation provisions in the Constitution and the following Consultation Act seem to be lacking in clarity at the procedural level. It was repeatedly expressed that there was a need for a revision of the cantonal consultation procedures on a statutory or regulation level.

Furthermore, the lack of clarity in delineating cantonal and federal powers in foreign policy mentioned above has an influence on the implementation of the bilateral agreements. Some of the agreements fall under the cantonal competences, in areas such as education, health, culture, infrastructure, public procurement and police and justice. The implementation of the Schengen agreement raises a number of practical questions relating to the role of the cantons in this process, for instance how the federal government can ensure that the provisions of Schengen are respected all over the country given that police powers, and thus responsibility for the implementation of much of the Schengen agreement, fall within the competence of the cantons.

5. The bilateral sectoral approach and the European Economic Area

5.1 Introduction

As a result of Bilaterals I and II, Switzerland is becoming more closely integrated with the European Union than any other non-EU member state except its three EFTA partners in the European Economic Area (EEA). Indeed, Bilaterals I and II were an explicit alternative to the EEA, following the rejection of the latter by the Swiss people, which itself was generally regarded as a stepping-stone towards full membership. This chapter compares the Swiss-EU bilateral relationship with those of the EFTA states in the EEA.[61]

Through the EEA agreement, Iceland, Liechtenstein and Norway are essentially part of the EU's Single Market, with the exception of the common policies on trade, agriculture and fisheries. The EEA also provides the framework for the participation of the EFTA states in dozens of EU programmes and the growing number of EU agencies. In addition, Iceland and in particular Norway are closely associated with the EU on foreign, security and defence policy, and in justice and home affairs through the Schengen and Dublin association agreements on border and asylum policy, respectively.[62] Indeed, the latter provided the model for Switzerland's Schengen and Dublin association agreements.

One unique feature of the EEA agreement is that it is multilateral, whereas the EU-Swiss agreements are bilateral, as are almost all other EU

---

[61] Vahl (2004).

[62] Emerson et al. (2002).

association agreements. However, the three EFTA states are required to speak with one voice, and from the EU's point of view, these agreements thus consist of two parties, similar to other association agreements. The difference from the associates' perspective is, however, profound, as it makes agreement on any issue dependent on acceptance by the other two EFTA states.

The EEA relationship differs considerably from the Swiss-EU bilateral sectoral approach also in its institutional set-up and in how the agreement is implemented. The 1999 Integration Report of the Swiss government raised a number of arguments for and against the bilateral approach as compared with the EEA. First, the latter was criticised for its institutional weakness, and the absence of the full right of co-decision. Secondly, the EEA was criticised for its content, as there is no customs union and the common agricultural and fisheries policies are not included, and nor are other important policy areas such as monetary policy, asylum, internal security, external policy. Third, the multilateral nature of the EEA and the concomitant obligation to speak with one voice was criticised.

The Integration Report identifies three main advantages of the sectoral approach based on the experiences in the negotiations of Bilateral I. First, it allows Switzerland an equal say with the EU in determining the subjects of negotiation. Secondly, the implementation takes place autonomously in Switzerland, and thirdly, the direct costs are low. One disadvantage of the sectoral approach highlighted in the report is a general reluctance on the part of the EU to engage in negotiations on new agreements, due to the diverse interests of the member states, which further ensures that negotiations, once launched, are lengthy. Successive EU enlargements have created a more complex Union with less flexibility in negotiating agreements with third countries. These difficulties are compounded by the systemic absence of Switzerland from meetings, which makes it difficult to clear up misunderstandings in a reasonable amount of time.

Opportunities for further rapprochement have been exhausted in the sectoral approach, according to the 1999 Integration Report. This would require the transfer of sovereign rights to the EU and acknowledging the supreme judicial authority of the European Court of Justice. Such steps might entail the elimination of the customs union frontier for trade in goods, equal and comprehensive cooperation on justice and home affairs, institutional safeguards for monetary and exchange rate stability and participation in economic agreements between the EU and other third countries. The sectoral approach also makes adjustments of the agreements to changing circumstances, e.g. technological improvements, cumbersome. This is particularly notable in the so-called 'mixed agreements' which require parliamentary approval in the EU member states.

5.2 Scope of the EEA

5.2.1 The core of the EEA

The provisions on the participation of the three EFTA states in the EU's internal market constitute the core of the EEA agreement. The scope of the EEA is determined by the existing EU *acquis* when the agreement was signed in 1992 plus the measures that have subsequently been adopted by the EU and to a very large extent also adopted by the EEA states. In total, more than 5,000 legal acts (Directives, Regulations and Decisions) have been incorporated into the EEA agreement since it entered into force 12 years ago.

Many of the agreements in Bilaterals I and II, as well as older agreements such as the 1972 free trade agreement, provide for Swiss access to the EU's internal market based on the principle of equivalent rules and standards. As seen above, regardless of whether or not the agreements make explicit reference to the *acquis*, EU-Swiss legal harmonisation in practice entails Swiss adoption of EU laws and regulations. The EEA currently consists of more than 1,500 directives, or approximately 95% of all EU internal market directives. How does this compare with the coverage of the EU-Swiss bilateral agreements?

It is beyond the scope of this study to find a precise answer to this question, which is also difficult to answer due to methodological challenges and the conceptual difference between the EEA and the bilateral sectoral approach. As far as methodology is concerned, clearly the importance of these directives and other instruments varies. Some are largely technical modifications to existing pieces of legislation, while others have a considerable political, economic and social impact on the countries concerned. Certain sectors and areas are covered by a large number of EU directives and regulations. For instance, approximately one-third of the EU's internal market directives are aimed at eliminating technical barriers to trade, which does not reflect their relative importance. It is difficult to envisage an analytical framework that is able to combine, compare and evaluate these different legislative acts to develop a precise 'measure' of the partial integration of non-EU member states with the EU.

Furthermore, the EEA and the bilateral sectoral agreements represent two conceptually different approaches towards the goal of ensuring access to the EU market for a third-country's companies and their products across a wide range of sectors, i.e. their partial inclusion in the Single Market. The EEA agreement is based on a comprehensive approach. It starts from the principle of the four freedoms enshrined in the Single Market, with detailed provisions for excluded sectors. The Swiss agreements are, by contrast, sector-specific agreements covering cooperation in specified areas, without reference to overarching principles like the four freedoms, and without including 'horizontal' and 'flanking' policies, such as EU competition and state aid policy, except in areas and sectors explicitly defined in the bilateral agreements.

In spite of these inherent difficulties, a number of observations can be made to give an indication of the overall scope of the EU-Swiss agreements compared with that of the EEA. Following the adoption of Bilateral II, Switzerland now has agreements covering a majority of the more than 30 chapters of the *acquis* used in accession negotiations. Many of the agreements include provisions related to several chapters of the *acquis*, notably the more comprehensive agreements such the one governing the free movement of persons.

The arguments supporting the EU's proposals for a financial contribution from Switzerland provide another indication of the scope of the EU-Swiss agreements compared with that of the EEA. According to the European Commission, the absence of an agreement on services entailed that the EU-Swiss bilateral agreements overall gave Switzerland access to roughly two-thirds of the internal market. The Commission therefore requested Switzerland to contribute two-thirds in per capita terms of the contribution of its EFTA partners in the EEA.

However, since the EEA agreement was negotiated, the *acquis* has developed significantly in areas beyond the internal market, notably through the ambitious integration underway in the field of justice and home affairs. This reduces the EEA's share of the *acquis*, which in the case of Norway and Iceland has been compensated for by the conclusion of agreements also in these areas, for instance Schengen/Dublin and Europol association agreements. Switzerland now finds itself in a similar situation following the conclusion of Schengen, Dublin and Europol agreements in the field of justice and home affairs.

5.2.2   Horizontal issues and cooperation beyond the four freedoms

The EEA agreement also provides for cooperation beyond the internal market and the four freedoms. The EFTA states and their citizens participate in EU programmes, including in the areas where Swiss participation is ensured through a bilateral agreement (or declaration of intent), such as research, the audio-visual sector, education and statistics, and are associated with a number of EU agencies through the EEA agreement, most recently the European Air Safety Agency (EASA). As in the case of Switzerland, the costs of participation of the EEA states in these programmes are covered by all participating states on the basis of their respective GDP/capita. Many of the agreements between the EU and Switzerland are concerned with participation in EU programmes and agencies. Swiss participation is however much less extensive than that of the EFTA states in the EEA. Switzerland currently participates only in a handful of EU programmes and agencies, while the EEA states participate in several dozens of EU programmes and are associated with almost half of the 18 EU agencies currently in operation.

Although the EU's common trade, agricultural and fisheries policies are excluded from the EEA agreement, there are important provisions covering these areas in the agreement, making it difficult to locate these sectors as being unambiguously either inside or outside the scope of the EEA agreement. Many of the greatest controversies surrounding the EEA agreement have been related to issues within these areas.

The EEA agreement does not cover the EU's Common Fisheries Policy. The agreement does however cover trade in certain fishery products divided by species and by degree of processing.[63] For a number of unprocessed fishery products, the EEA gives the EFTA states free access to the EU market, while it stipulates higher tariffs for processed products. This situation stimulates the export of raw materials to be processed in the EU. For so-called 'sensitive products', the EU has kept high tariffs, including, among others, on salmon, which constitutes almost half of

---

[63] See Protocol 9 of the EEA agreement, which covers fisheries.

Norway's fish exports to the EU. This has become the main source of friction between the EU and Norway in the fisheries sector. Norway has frequently been forced to introduce voluntary export constraints following demands by EU fish farmers, stalling the growth in Norwegian exports and reducing Norway's market share in the fast-growing EU market.

Although the EEA agreement does not include the Common Agricultural Policy, and agricultural products are explicitly excluded from the general provision on the free movement of goods within the EEA, it does contain important provisions of relevance to the agricultural sector in the EFTA countries. The key provisions are found in Annex I, which brings the EU *acquis* on veterinary standards into the EEA agreement, Protocol 3 on trade in processed agricultural products and Art. 19, which stipulates the progressive liberalisation of trade in agricultural goods and which is to be reviewed every other year.[64] Some of the most controversial issues relating to the EEA agreement at the moment relate to veterinary standards, in particular, EU rules and standards concerning additives in food and on genetically modified organisms. For different reasons, however, most of these provisions have not yet, or only quite recently, entered into force, so that the full impact of the EEA agreement on Norway's agricultural sector has not yet been felt. Trade in processed agricultural products was the main unresolved issue when the EEA agreement was signed in the spring of 1992, and the relevant protocol (Protocol 3) has only been in force since January 2002. Only one review of trade liberalisation, as stipulated by Art. 19 of the EEA agreement, took place in the first eight years after entry into force, partially because such a review was linked by the Norwegian side to agreement on Protocol 3.

The EEA is not a customs union and there is no formal linkages concerning trade policy with third parties. The EFTA states are therefore theoretically free to determine their own external trade policy. In practice, however, the scope for divergence from the EU policies is fairly limited. This is seen in regional or bilateral trade relations, where EFTA followed a policy of 'shadowing' the EU in concluding agreements with third countries. The first agreements were initiated in the 1990s with the Central and East European economies, aimed at preventing or limiting any trade diversion or discrimination resulting from the Europe agreements between

---

[64] Chapter 2 of the EEA agreement covers agricultural and fisheries products.

the EU and these countries. EFTA has concluded more than a dozen such agreements, including with countries in the Western Balkans, the Mediterranean, and selected countries in America and Asia, in some cases concluding agreements ahead of the EU. The scope of the EFTA free trade agreements is more or less the same as the coverage of the EU bilaterals with the countries concerned. Differences occur mainly in those sectors that are not fully covered, such as agriculture where there are bilateral protocols between each EFTA state and the free trade partner of EFTA. Most of these are with relative insignificant trading partners of the EFTA countries, comprising in total approximately 4% of the total trade of the EFTA members. However, the EFTA states have recently become more proactive in this trade diplomacy, concluding free trade agreements before the EU concludes similar agreements, most recently seen with the EFTA agreement with South Korea. This is also taking place bilaterally, the most prominent example being the bilateral exploratory talks between Switzerland and the US begun in mid-2005 on a possible US-Swiss free trade agreement.

5.3 Institutional framework

5.3.1 The institutions of the EEA

The institutional framework established to manage the EEA agreement differs considerably from that of the bilateral agreements between Switzerland and the EU. In some respects, for instance its institutional structure, it is more typical of EU agreements with other third countries than the agreements between the EU and Switzerland. The institutions of the EEA include a high-level political body, *the EEA Council*, a committee of senior officials, *the EEA Joint Committee*, an advisory parliamentary committee, *the EEA Joint Parliamentary Committee*, and a consultative body for the social partners, *the EEA Consultative Committee*. Most EU third-country agreements have a similar structure of a high-level political council, a committee of senior officials and a parliamentary committee.

The *EEA Council* is the main political body of the EEA. It consists of "members of the Council of the European Communities and members of the European Commission, and of one member of the Government of each of the EFTA States" (Art. 90), and meets twice per year. It provides political impetus to the agreement and guidelines for the Joint Committee, evaluates the functioning of the EEA agreement, as well as being a forum for general consultations on international affairs. In terms of institutional framework, the absence of a counterpart to this political forum is one of the main differences between the EEA and the EU-Swiss bilateral agreements.

The *EEA Joint Committee* is responsible for the day-to-day management of the EEA agreement, and is thus the equivalent to the bilateral EU-Swiss joint committees. It consists of the EU ambassadors of the EFTA states and representatives of the European Commission and takes decisions by consensus on incorporation of EU legislation into the agreement. It is assisted by five subcommittees: i) free movement of goods, ii) free movement of capital, iii) free movement of persons, iv) horizontal and flanking policies and v) legal and institutional matters, as well as ad hoc expert and working groups.

The EEA Joint Committee meets every month, which is far more frequent than any other senior officials committee of EU and third-country officials. Annual meetings, such as in the EU-Swiss joint committees, is the norm in EU external relations. But with the entry into force of Bilateral II, there will be more than 20 joint committees and an even greater number of subcommittees between the EU and Switzerland. The institutional framework of the EU-Swiss agreements thus provides for more formal meetings between EU and Swiss senior officials than the EEA agreement.

The *Joint Parliamentary Committee* (JPC) consists of 66 members, half from the European Parliament and half from the national parliaments of the EEA countries, and meets twice per year. The JPC plays a modest role in the EEA. Its contribution comes through 'dialogue and debate' and through reports and resolutions adopted by the JPC. It examines the annual report of the EEA Joint Committee, and has the right to call the President of the EEA Council to appear before them and be heard by the JPC. The annual 'bilateral' meetings between representatives of the European Parliament and national parliaments of the EFTA countries of the EEA initiated in the 1980s have continued in parallel with the JPC.

Delegates from the Swiss Federal Parliament and the European Parliament have also held annual meetings since the early 1980s. However, the Swiss federal parliament plays no formal role in the bilateral EU-Swiss agreements of the kind their EFTA counterparts in the EEA do through the JPC, although Swiss parliamentarians benefit from their participation as observers in the EEA Joint Parliamentary Committee.

The *EEA Consultative Committee* is composed of representatives of social partners/economic and social interest groups, and comprises an equal number of members of the EFTA Consultative Committee and the

Economic and Social Committee of the EU (ECOSOC). It works to strengthen contacts between the social partners and provides input to the work of the EEA in the form of reports and resolutions.

In addition to the regular institutions of EU third-country agreements, specific institutions with competencies limited to the EFTA (i.e. non-EU) members of the EEA agreement were also established, creating a 'two-pillar' institutional structure that is unique among EU third-country agreements. This was necessary in order to reconcile the central aim of maintaining a homogenous legal area with the constitutional and political requirements of the EEA states, which prevented them from accepting direct decisions by the European Commission or the European Court of Justice, as well as safeguarding the autonomy of EU decision-making.

The *EFTA Surveillance Authority* (ESA) was established to ensure that the EEA states fulfil their obligations under the EEA agreement, i.e. that the provisions of the agreement are properly implemented in the national legal orders of the EEA member states and correctly applied by the authorities. It thus performs a similar role as does the European Commission vis-à-vis the EU member states. Cases are either initiated by the ESA itself or on the basis of complaints from individual legal persons or the Commission. The ESA has wider powers in the fields of public procurement, competition and state aid.[65] The Brussels-based ESA is led by a college with one member from each of the three EEA members and has a staff of almost 50 officials, approximately two-thirds of whom are from the EEA countries.

The *EFTA Court* in Luxembourg exercises similar competencies with respect to the EEA states as the European Court of Justice does vis-à-vis the EU member states. It deals with infringement cases brought by the ESA against an EEA state with regard to EEA implementation, the settlement of disputes between EEA states, appeals concerning decisions taken by the ESA, and gives advisory opinions to national courts on the interpretation of

---

[65] In the field of public procurement, the ESA has the right to directly request that infringements are corrected; on competition, the power to make on-the-spot inspections, issue Statement of Objections ordering eventual infringements of competition provisions to be brought to an end, and in case of non-compliance, to impose fines; and in the area of state aid, to initiate and conduct investigations concerning state aid measures

EEA rules. The Court, consisting of three judges appointed for six years, one from each of the EEA countries, only sits in plenary session and its decisions are taken by majority vote. The Court has a staff of 12, in addition to the three judges.

In order to prepare and coordinate their positions in the joint EEA bodies, the *Standing Committee of the EFTA states* was established. It consists of representatives from Iceland, Liechtenstein and Norway, and observers from Switzerland and the ESA. The Standing Committee has a structure of five subcommittees and a number of working groups mirroring that of the EEA Joint Committee, and is assisted by a staff of approximately 40 in Brussels.

The EEA agreement is then by far the most complex and structured of all EU association and cooperation agreements. However, the burden of maintaining this complicated machinery is mainly taken care of by the EEA states. They are responsible for the running of the EFTA bodies specifically established for the EEA agreement, leaving the Commission and the ECJ to concentrate on the EU member states.

5.3.2 Decision-shaping and decision-making

According to Art. 99 of the EEA agreement, the European Commission must seek the advice from EFTA experts in the same way it seeks advice from experts in the EU member states. Art. 100 calls on the Commission to ensure "as wide a participation as possible" in the preparatory stage of draft measures and that it refers to these experts on an equal basis with EU experts when drafting such measures. This entails that experts and officials from the EFTA states participate in the preparatory phases of the legislative process in more than 200 Commission committees. It should here be noted that the European Commission and the EFTA states disagree on the precise extent of the legal right of participation in Commission comitology committees. This is in any case a challenging and resource-intensive process for the EEA states, since they must work quickly if they are to consult with domestic interests in order to represent national interests effectively. Some officials claimed that the existence of the EFTA Secretariat was an important reason why the EEA functions smoothly. Although the EFTA Secretariat helps in the process of identifying issues, there is still a danger that EEA positions are not firmly established in time. However, the Commission will often engage in a fairly lengthy consultation procedure, taking the form of green and white papers, which helps facilitate inputs from all interests, including the EEA states.

Liaison between the EFTA Secretariat and the Commission also helps to facilitate EFTA input, but there would appear to be a lack of consistency on the Commission side in the approach and effort made by different services. Each DG designates an office to deal with the EEA dimension of any proposed measures, but many of these officials have extensive other responsibilities and cannot always devote much time to monitoring everything that goes on in the DG and passing this information to the EFTA Secretariat.

By contrast, the Swiss agreements allow for much more limited participation by Swiss experts in these committees. This is due to the sector-specific approach and that, with the exception of the field of civil aviation, the agreements do not amount to a wholesale adoption of the *acquis*. However, in connection with the conclusion of the Bilateral I package, the EU Council of Ministers adopted a declaration granting Swiss representatives the right to participate as observers with a right to speak, but not to vote, in committee meetings in the areas of research, air transport, social security and recognition of diplomas. In addition, the Commission is committed to consult with Swiss experts on an equal basis with experts from EU member states in fields where Swiss legislation is recognised as equivalent to the *acquis*. Switzerland also benefits from its observer status in the EFTA Standing Committee, which coordinates the position of the three EFTA EEA states on EEA matters.

It was acknowledged by several interlocutors that the EFTA members of the EEA were more involved in the earlier phases in the development of EU legislation than their Swiss counterparts. A frequent opinion voiced by Swiss officials was that Switzerland would only be invited to participate in a committee or working group as an expert in a specific area. This was seen as a key deficiency of the bilateral sectoral approach. Some EU officials noted that in practice, Swiss officials are frequently invited on an informal ad hoc basis, and that the difference vis-à-vis the EFTA states in the EEA was in practice not that significant.

The influence exerted by the non-member states in the decision-shaping phases also depends of course on how the state itself organises its internal processes and the resources committed to the process. In the case of Norway, both the government and the parliament have come under criticism recently. A report from the Auditor General, for example criticised the Norwegian government and central administration for not taking full advantage of the opportunities available for decision-shaping under the EEA agreement. Another study analysing the debate on the EU and new EU legislation in the Norwegian and Swedish parliaments found that the latter spends much more time debating the EU and new EEA relevant EU law than do its Norwegian counterpart.[66]

It is also a result of broader developments in the relationship between the main EU institutions. Because of the shifting balance between the EU institutions, with a strengthening of the Council of Ministers and the European Parliament at the expense of the Commission and national parliaments, such participation in EU decision-shaping is however becoming less significant. The Council and its working groups play an increasingly important role in shaping EC legislation, as does the European Parliament with the extension of 'co-decision' in recent treaties. The growing use of other policy-making methods such as the 'open co-ordination' of the Lisbon process, in which the Council machinery plays the pivotal role, both exemplifies and further exacerbates the shifting balance among the EU institutions. Some EU officials interviewed questioned the importance of such participation in EU 'decision-shaping' in general. Because these countries are not member states, officials from the member states and the EU institutions do not, in the end, have to take their views and positions into account reaching a decision.

Once the drafting of a legislative measure begins, the EEA states are excluded from the process. Short of full membership of the EU, the EEA members cannot have a vote. Indeed, no EU association or cooperation agreement with a non-member allows any significant participation of representatives of the associated states in the decision-making process in the EU. The arrangement closest to being an exception to this is the Schengen association agreements with Iceland, Norway, and now Switzerland. Through the so-called 'Mixed Committee', the associated states participate in what is in effect the Justice and Home Affairs Council, COREPER and the Council working groups relating to the Schengen agreement. Switzerland is granted the right to make 'suggestions' in the Mixed Committee, but does not have a vote, and the right to propose and adopt new acts is reserved to the EU and its member states (Art. 4 (4)).

---

[66] See Riksrevisjonen (2005) and Melsæter & Sverdrup (2004).

But there are a range of indirect means whereby EFTA views can be fed into the process. First of all, there is not always a clear de facto distinction between the work of a Commission expert advisory committee and a drafting committee of the Council. Suggestions for possible approaches to drafting may well be discussed in the expert groups. During the Council discussions, the EFTA Secretariat can retain some contact with what is going on via the Commission which may feed in EFTA views. The EFTA Secretariat can also maintain contact with the Council Secretariat in order to keep abreast of developments. They can of course also attempt to exert some influence through bilateral diplomacy with EU member states, an avenue that is open to Switzerland as well.

5.4   Incorporation and implementation of new *acquis*

The EEA is the primary example of a dynamic agreement, with detailed provisions for the inclusion of new EU *acquis* into the agreement. Monthly meetings at senior officials level takes binding decisions by consensus on the incorporation of new rules and regulations into the EEA agreement, through their adoption in the national law of the non-EU EEA member states. In recent years, the number of legal acts incorporated into the agreement has hovered at around 300 per year.[67]

As in the joint committees of the EU-Swiss bilateral agreements, adoption of any EU legislation or other provision into the EEA requires agreement in the Joint Committee of the EEA (Art. 93). In this sense, the EEA does not differ from the EU-Swiss agreements, or any other EU agreements with third countries, although the EFTA states in the EEA are required to speak with one voice, which is rare in EU agreements with third countries. Furthermore, the EEA includes provisions granting the EFTA states the option of opting out of any EU legislation for the EEA states as a group. This 'right of reservation', known colloquially but misleadingly as a 'veto-right', has not been used to date. If such action were however to be taken by either the three EEA states (which have to speak on this as in other EEA matters with one voice) or the EU side, the ensuing dispute could take several courses. If agreement concerning the

---

[67] 201 legal acts in 2000, 401 in 2001, 324 in 2002, 298 in 2003 and 309 in 2004 (EFTA Secretariat Annual Report, various years).

incorporation of secondary legislation into the EEA *acquis* is not found in the Joint Committee, the parties may then request the ECJ for an interpretation of the relevant rule (Art. 111). If this fails to lead to a solution, the outcome is either that a) the affected part of the treaty is suspended (Art. 102); b) the introduction of 'safeguard measures' by one of the contracting parties, which could lead to counter-measures by other parties (Arts 112-114); or, as a last resort, c) withdrawal from the EEA agreement.

As with the existing *acquis*, the EEA states seem committed to adopting all new areas of *acquis*. This appears to be because the moves towards liberalisation represented by the EU *acquis* are generally in line with the national interests of the countries concerned. Such general support for the approach of the EU should not, however, disguise a number of quite important issues and tensions between the EEA states and the EU when it comes to extending the EU *acquis*.

The EFTA Surveillance Authority (ESA) has responsibility for ensuring the effective and timely implementation of the decision of the Joint Committee. It produces a biannual scoreboard on implementation of the EEA *acquis*, mirroring the scoreboard produced by the Commission on implementation of the internal market *acquis* in the EU. While there have been several instances where the EFTA states' implementation of the *acquis* has been late or below the EU average, for much of the time since the entry into force of the EEA more than a decade ago, the EFTA states' implementation record has been comfortably above the EU average. According to the 16th Internal Market Scoreboard for the EFTA states from the ESA of July 2005, the Implementation (or transposition) deficit of the three EFTA states in the EEA is lower than the average in the EU (1.4% and 1.9%, respectively).

In terms of the transposition process, the EEA and its 'fast-track' procedures for implementing new *acquis* were regarded positively compared with the long and unwieldy transposition process in EU-Swiss relations. The difference with the EEA was also noted by Swiss officials, who stated that a frequent Swiss position was to wait for EU member states, noticeably countries such as Germany and the Netherlands, to see how they implemented new *acquis* before venturing to do so at home.

Complaints that the ESA takes an increasingly legalistic view of the agreement, and that they are less tolerant of special demands from the three EEA states, are increasingly heard among politicians in the EFTA member states. It is frequently seen as playing a more pro-active role than initially envisaged and is criticised for its broad interpretations of the scope of the EEA agreement.[68] The steadily growing number of ESA 'own initiatives' supports the view that the ESA is becoming gradually more pro-active. Another explanation is that so far, most cases have been concerned with less controversial issues related to the free movement of goods, whereas until quite recently there had been relatively few cases in more controversial fields such as financial services, competition and state aid, reflecting the gradual completion of the single market programme also in these areas. That the complaints about the EEA all related to how the agreement has developed over time illustrate the importance of keeping in mind that comparisons between the EEA and the EU-Swiss bilateral agreements are hampered by the fact that Bilateral I only entered into force in June 2002, and that most of these have significant periods of transition before they are fully implemented.

The ESA and the EFTA Court provide the second pillar of the EEA. EU institutions such as the Commission and the Court have no authority vis-à-vis the EFTA states of the EEA similar to that accorded to them in Switzerland by the air transport agreement. Whilst this is the case from a legal point of view, the practical outcome is that the EEA still adopts the EU *acquis*. In order to ensure the credibility of a single market spanning across the whole of the EEA, a homogeneous market, the ESA has to follow the approach adopted by the Commission when it comes to interpreting any piece of legislation. Material circumstances can differ and so the ESA and Commission positions may diverge from time to time, but close cooperation between the Commission and ESA has ensured that there is no different interpretation of the rules. On the rare occasion when the ESA might be in a position to set a precedent not yet covered by the EU *acquis*, the Commission has called for and obtained restraint from the ESA.

5.5   The settlement of disputes

In most EU agreements with third countries, the settlement of disputes takes place in the bilateral committee of senior officials, with final arbitration left to a ministerial council, or, as in the case of the EU-Swiss

---

[68] See Nei til EU (2001).

agreements, to a Joint or Mixed Committee. Although this is also, ultimately, the case in the EEA agreement, a more elaborate dispute settlement mechanism has been established. A special court, the EFTA Court, was established to deal with infringement cases and for the settlement of disputes between the EFTA EEA states. As in the EU-Swiss agreements, there is no direct effect in the EFTA states as in the EU, but ECJ case law and the decisions of the EFTA court must be taken into account. Most issues are solved through these legal procedures.[69] Few cases even go as far as the EFTA Court, and in the first nine years after the entry into force of the EEA, disputes were only been brought back to the EEA Council twice.

The EFTA Court is also available for the review of any ESA decision or for redress in the case of non-implementation by an EEA state. Between five and ten cases annually have been decided by the EFTA Court in recent years.[70] This compares with the more than 1,000 cases being brought to the ECJ and the EU Court of First Instance annually, most of which are of relevance to the single market. Thus, the flow of case law affecting the EEA comes predominantly from the EU.

5.6   Conclusions

Overall, the scope of the EU-Swiss bilateral agreements falls short of the EEA, although there are some exceptions, notably the air transport agreement. The former only entails partial access to the EU's internal market, notably without an agreement on services. The EEA states also participate much more extensively in EU programmes and agencies than does Switzerland. This seems in line with the Commission's argument following the Swiss rejection of the EEA that "it would be inappropriate for

---

[69] According to the Norwegian EEA expert Fredrik Sejersted, "when the EEA agreement is signed, politics is over. Now the rest is only law." Quoted in Claes & Tranøy (1999, p. V).

[70] It made rulings on nine cases in 2000, six in 2001, nine in 2002, five in 2003, five in 2004 and eight cases in 2005. Among the latter, two were requests for advisory opinions, three were actions brought by the ESA, one brought by an EFTA state and two actions were brought to the ETA Court by (groups) of EFTA companies.

Switzerland to obtain all the advantages of an Agreement which it has rejected".[71]

In the EEA, the cost of obtaining guaranteed market access to the European single market has been a reduced scope for national policy autonomy in the policy areas covered by the EU *acquis*. Experience has shown the limited influence of the EFTA states in case of disputes. And although the EEA states can opt out, there has so far been no case in which this has actually happened, because of the perception that the homogeneity of the market depends on the credibility of the tie with the EU *acquis*. In practical terms, therefore, the EEA states have had to adopt the whole *acquis*, similar to the more limited experience of Bilaterals I and II. The EU has also been careful to discourage any notion of the possibility to 'cherry-pick' the *acquis* in its relations with Switzerland as well. Indeed, this trend has strengthened during the period when Bilaterals I and II were negotiated.

Institutional weakness, which was another criticism levied against the EEA in the 1999 Integration Report, is arguably even more characteristic of EU-Swiss agreements, and is therefore an important reason why the issue of an association agreement has been raised (see below). The EEA seems to provide greater opportunities for 'decision-shaping' than the bilateral sectoral approach, although there are clear limits to this and there are no co-decision rights. This observation has to be qualified, however, by the fact that Bilateral I has only been in force for little more than three-and-a-half years at the time of writing and it may simply be too early to tell. The legislative process in the EU – from the time an issue makes it onto the EU agenda to the enactment of new legislation – is often considerably longer than this.

The obligation to speak with one voice does impose further constraints on national autonomy, and would be an important factor in case any of the three EFTA EEA states would desire to exercise the 'right of reservation', which would require negotiations among the three EFTA partners in the EEA. This has been a limited problem among the three EFTA states of the EEA, although there seems to be a tendency for Norway to be most positive towards the inclusion of new *acquis* into the agreement.

---

[71] European Commission (1993).

There were also some criticisms of Norway during the negotiations of the financial contribution in 2003, as its EFTA partners found it too willing to substantially increase the funding provided by the three EFTA states. This was resolved by creating a special Norwegian financial facility through which approximately half of the funds are channelled, the result of which is that Liechtenstein and Iceland contribute about half of Norway's contribution to the EU in per capita terms.

While there have been minor disputes on incorporation of new *acquis* in the EEA, a perhaps bigger challenge has been the perception that the scope of the EEA agreement has been gradually expanded over time, and that the institutions established to manage the agreement have exceeded their authority in interpreting the agreement. Similar concerns, in particular relating to the scope of the agreement, have appeared also in EU-Swiss relations and the agreements of Bilaterals I and II. The lesson from the EEA on this issue seems to be that such problems are likely to increase rather than diminish over time, and are thus likely to constitute a growing challenge for Switzerland.

The sectoral approach has not prevented Switzerland from entering into commitments with the EU that it initially did not seek, such as the agreement on taxation of savings and the financial contribution. Another purported benefit of the bilateral sectoral approach was that the direct costs were low. The financial contribution significantly reduces the strength of this argument, although the costs remain far below Switzerland's likely net contribution to the EU in case it were to become an EU member.

Another purported problem with the sectoral approach cited by the 1999 Integration Report was that the EU would be very reluctant to enter into new agreements, and that negotiations of such agreements would be lengthy due to the diversity of interests within the EU. It has indeed taken more than a decade to conclude the agreements sought by Switzerland after the rejection of the EEA in December 1992. The expectations that a larger Union would be less flexible in terms of exceptions and derogations have also been borne out in practice, with the EU adopting a more restrictive policy against permanent exceptions during the process leading up to the EU enlargement in 2004.

The existence of a two-pillar system in the EEA seems to serve more of a political purpose in limiting the loss of formal sovereignty by EEA states, rather than to increase their national policy autonomy. In the EU-Swiss agreement, this political purpose is served with reference to 'equivalence of law' rather than 'adoption of the *acquis*' and the autonomous implementation of the agreements in Switzerland. But as former External Relations Commissioner Chris Patten, who was responsible for the management of the EEA as well as the negotiations on Bilaterals I and II, concludes:

> They enjoyed all the enhanced sovereignty that comes with staying at home while the decisions that intimately affect their own economic life are made by their neighbours in Brussels. We put a diplomatic gloss on it of course. But to enjoy our markets, they have to follow our rules; rules that they do not make or share in making. … When we enlarged the Union, these outer-ring countries had to pay into the funds that we make available to help the poorer new members. I remember a Swiss negotiator telephoning me to plead that this subscription should be presented as a voluntary donation for development in the deprived parts of Europe, not an additional fee for access to a larger market. I was happy to oblige. But we both knew what the truth was. *De facto* sovereignty or *de jure*?[72]

---

[72] Patten (2005, p. 83).

6. The prospects for relations between the EU and Switzerland

The overall conclusion of this study is that so far, three and a half years after the entry into force, the Bilateral I package of sector-specific agreements between the EU and Switzerland is functioning well. There have been no significant conflicts between the two sides and although there have been a few minor disputes on some of the agreements, all of these have been resolved in a friendly manner.

Their ability to find amicable solutions and willingness to use the institutional framework of the bilateral agreements indicate a broad commonality of interest between the EU and Switzerland. Significant changes in the EU in important areas for EU-Swiss relations, for instance on free movement of persons, air transport and Schengen cooperation in the wake of the September 11, 2001 terrorist attacks, have been handled smoothly between the EU and Switzerland.

Furthermore, the two parties seem content with the bilateral sectoral approach. Although the Swiss application has only been 'frozen' and not withdrawn, there is broad agreement among the political parties in Switzerland that the bilateral sectoral approach is the only viable alternative in the foreseeable future. This appears to be supported by the Swiss public. There have been three referenda on Bilaterals I and II, all of which have been supported by the Swiss people, while the most recent proposal to re-activate the membership application in 2001 was firmly rejected (77% against). The Swiss parliament has twice rejected motions to withdraw the Swiss membership application. Important Swiss actors, such as the industry association *Economiesuisse*, which previously supported EU membership for Switzerland, are now, following the conclusion of Bilaterals I and II, content with the bilateral sectoral approach currently pursued by the Swiss government.[73] Most interlocutors agreed that it was now time to implement Bilaterals I and II and allow them to operate for at least a few years before any debate on more fundamental alternatives to the bilateral sectoral approach is contemplated. A first official assessment is expected in a new comprehensive report on Switzerland and the EU to be prepared by the Swiss government in 2006.

6.1   Full implementation of Bilateral I and Bilateral II

The entry into force and full implementation of Bilateral II as well as of Bilateral I will be a major preoccupation in EU- Swiss relations well into the next decade.

As there is no guillotine clause in Bilateral II apart from the link between Schengen and Dublin, the entry into force of the nine agreements will be on an individual basis. Three of the nine agreements in Bilateral II – on processed agricultural products, taxation on savings and pensions – entered into force in 2005. It is expected that the Schengen association agreement might enter into force in early 2006. But Switzerland is behind the new member states in the queue to join the Schengen area. The latter is expected to occur in the second half of 2007, which would mean that the Schengen association agreement would be fully implemented and border controls lifted in early 2008.

Although the incorporation of new *acquis* into the Schengen association agreement requires Swiss consent, the fact that such a rejection entails the termination of the entire agreement increases the stakes and makes it unlikely that Switzerland will oppose any new measures. While this seems clear to Swiss officials, they do not expect this to become a big problem, as they do not foresee any significant new Schengen-relevant *acquis* as emerging in coming years.

Swiss officials have participated in the Schengen association institutions since the signing of the agreement in October 2004. This includes participation in more than 30 working groups in the Commission, both in the preparatory phase of legislation and on implementation, and in

---

[73] See remarks of the Economiesuisse President (Ramsauer, 2005).

the Council managing the Schengen and Dublin conventions. There are indications that the Swiss take a more cautious line in the Mixed Committee on whether or not new *acquis* in the justice and home affairs field is 'Schengen-relevant' than the position taken by the other Schengen associates Norway and Iceland. On the future development of Schengen and the eventual adoption of new legislation in Switzerland, some Swiss officials did not expect any significant developments to the Schengen *acquis*, and were thus rather dismissive of suggestions that this represented an important challenge in the years ahead. This seems a rather sanguine view, particularly in light of the conclusion of the Treaty of Prüm among seven EU member states in May 2005. This treaty aims to enhance cooperation on Schengen-relevant issues and although it was concluded outside the EU framework. The expectation is that this will eventually be part of the Schengen regime of the EU.[74]

The entry into force of the rest of the agreements of Bilateral II is expected in 2006 in the case of the agreements on environment and MEDIA or in 2007, in the case of the statistics agreement. This will then be followed by the establishment of a further six bilateral committees, which will first need to establish their own rules of procedure.

New *acquis* and other developments in the EU will also have to be handled in the more dynamic agreements. In air transport, there is still a backlog of legislation to be incorporated into the agreement, although this has recently been reduced. A consolidated version of the Air Transport agreement including the amendments made since entry into force in 2002 is to be made available to the public in 2006.

6.2   Future agreements

The conclusion of Bilateral II does not spell the end of the development of EU-Swiss contractual relations. A series of further bilateral agreements between the EU and Switzerland are 'in the pipeline', and one can expect a number of adaptations to existing agreements, as the EU continues to evolve.

---

[74] Balzacq et al. (2006).

6.2.1   Agreements under discussion

A number of potential bilateral agreements are under discussion between Switzerland and the EU. These include agreements providing for Swiss participation in EU programmes and agencies and further sectoral agreements. There have also been talks on Swiss participation in the EU's GALILEO satellite navigation project and Swiss association with the European Food Safety Agency. On education, Switzerland has shown an interest in participating in the European Centre for the Development of Vocational Training and EURYDICE, the European educational information network. Switzerland also seeks some sort of participation in the recently established European Railway Safety Agency.

The EU and Switzerland are also negotiating a framework agreement on the financial and legal aspects of Swiss participation in ESDP operations. Switzerland participates in several EU operations, with both civilian and military personnel, for instance in the EU Police Mission and the military operation (EUFOR) in Bosnia-Herzegovina, the monitoring mission in Aceh, Indonesia and participated in the now completed Operation Proxima in Macedonia. This has so far taken place on the basis of ad hoc agreements negotiated for each operation.

There have also been talks on electricity issues, such as transit and market access. The EU's main concern is the need to improve the Swiss electricity grid, seen as an important cause behind the blackout in Italy in 2002. Switzerland recently amended its legislation in line with the standards of the Florence Electricity Regulators Forum. Switzerland on its side is interested in obtaining access to the liberalised EU market. According to EU officials, it is not difficult to envisage additional topics that may lead to the conclusion of subsequent agreements.

In light of the previous bundling of negotiations into packages, one question that arose in the interviews was whether a Bilateral III package is contemplated. The short answer to this question was a unanimous 'no' from the EU and Swiss officials interviewed. This method yields a lengthy and cumbersome negotiation process and can easily be regarded as an unreasonable approach insofar as cooperation in one area may become entirely dependent upon cooperation (or lack thereof) on a completely unrelated dossier.

Indeed, Bilateral I may turn out to be an exception born of exceptional circumstances following the Swiss rejection of the EEA and subsequent request for a somewhat 'lighter' alternative in the shape of a set of sectoral agreements. The trend away from package negotiations emerged in the period between negotiations over the two sets of agreements, evidenced in the fact that Bilateral II was in several respects less of a set package than Bilateral I. While the agreements of Bilateral II were signed at the same time, the launch of negotiations were staggered, with negotiations on four dossiers starting in 2001, followed by another four dossiers in mid-2002 and a final dossier towards the end of that year. More importantly, there is no 'guillotine clause' linking the agreements of Bilateral II, apart from the linkage between the Schengen and Dublin accords.

6.2.2   Outstanding issues

There are also two outstanding issues from the Bilateral II talks that have not been resolved. First, Switzerland and the EU have not agreed as of early 2006 on the Swiss financial contribution. Although agreement was reached in principle in autumn 2003, the main outstanding issue concerns whether parts of the Swiss contribution will be allocated to 'old' but less prosperous EU member states such as Greece, Spain and Portugal. The contribution was initially intended for the 2005-09 period, but with the delay the five-year period is now from late 2006 to 2011.

The second outstanding issue concerns an agreement on services, which was initially part of the negotiations of Bilateral II. After a few rounds of negotiations, however, it became clear that the positions of the two parties were too far apart. It was in the course of these negotiations that the EU began to manifest its reluctance to tolerate exceptions to the *acquis*. The EU did not agree with the Swiss proposal for a more limited agreement covering only certain specified sectors, and insisted on a broad agreement including EU competition policy and company law, as well as flanking policies, the inclusion of which is difficult to delineate. An agreement on the EU's terms would, according to EU officials, require further reforms of the services sector in Switzerland to comply with EU competition policies.

It was thus decided in March 2003 that since it would not be possible to conclude an agreement in parallel with the other agreements of Bilateral II, negotiations would be put on hold and resumed at a later unspecified date. Both Swiss and EU officials contend that such an agreement will eventually be concluded, although neither side appears to envisage the resumption of negotiations in the foreseeable future. The issue is further complicated by the fact that the single market in services is far from completed, and that the required legislation is highly politically sensitive within the EU. It seems unlikely that negotiations with Switzerland will resume before some of the key pending pieces, such as the services directive, have been adopted by the EU.

6.2.3 Expected adaptations to existing agreements

There are also likely to be negotiations on amendments to existing agreements. A new protocol on the free movement of persons extending the agreement to also cover Romania and Bulgaria is likely to be negotiated from 2006 onward, and will in due course be followed by further protocols when (or if) the EU enlarges further.

Swiss participation in EU programmes negotiated in Bilaterals I and II will have to be re-negotiated as the multi-year programmes expire. This is relevant for the research agreement with the expiry of the 6th Framework Programme and the audio-visual agreement with the expiry of the MEDIA programmes, both at the end of 2006.

Amendments to the agriculture agreement are also in the pipeline, in particular a protocol on mutual protection of labels for protected geographic indications. This had been on the Swiss list in 1993 and the negotiation of this protocol was envisaged in a joint declaration made during the signing of Bilateral I in 1999.

Issues related to earlier agreements are also likely to arise. One such issue concerns the corporate tax regimes. In late 2005, the European Commission raised the question whether certain corporate tax regimes in certain Swiss cantons should be considered 'predatory' in the context of the 1972 agreement. Switzerland contends that this is not covered by the agreement. The matter is as of early 2006 subject to an intensive dialogue between the EU and Switzerland including at the ministerial level.[75]

---

[75] See for instance "No breakthrough in Swiss-EU tax dispute" (downloaded from www.swisspolitics.org, dated 15 December 2005) and "Swiss defend corporate tax regime", *Financial Times*, 14 February 2006.

6.2.4   Other developments

The Europeanisation of Switzerland is likely to continue beyond the further development of contractual relations between Switzerland and the EU. As long as Eurolex remains, Swiss legislation will become ever more EU compatible, regardless of the direct implications of existing and future bilateral agreements.

Further unilateral measures of Europeanisation can be expected. The *Cassis de Dijon* principle, which applies to non-harmonised products in the single European market and which is extended to the EEA, is not included in the agreement on technical barriers to trade between the EU and Switzerland. However, the Federal Council has decided to open the Swiss market – in accordance with the *Cassis de Dijon* principle to products circulating freely within the EU – even if the EU as such has no plans to reciprocate. The Swiss State Secretariat for Economic Affairs (SECO) is therefore currently preparing a revision of the federal statute of technical barriers to trade. The interested groups will be consulted in spring 2006 followed by a plenum debate in the Federal Assembly towards the end of the year. It seemed at the time of writing likely that the principle would be adopted with important caveats, notably excluding territorial application of intellectual property rights, which would reduce the impact of its unilateral adoption by Switzerland.

6.3   Adaptations to the bilateral sectoral approach

6.3.1   The idea of an association agreement

The idea of a framework association agreement was raised in the public discourse by Swiss officials in spring 2005.[76] The idea of an association treaty "going beyond the content of the EEA ... specifically tailored to suit Switzerland" was raised briefly in the 1999 Integration Report. It was however dismissed, as it "presupposes a willingness of the EU to negotiate in this sense and fails to recognise that only EU Member States can exercise rights of co-decision". The need for improved coordination of EU-Swiss relations to improve the functioning of the bilateral agreements and the

---

[76] See "Cabinet weighs alternatives to EU membership" in www.swisspolitics.org, quoting interview with State Secretary Michael Ambühl of the Integration Bureau, dated 19 June 2005.

activities of the joint committees has been discussed much in recent months, and is apparently to be examined further by European and Swiss experts.[77]

EU officials seemed to think that the idea of an association agreement was raised by Swiss officials in part as a potential replacement for the existing bilateral agreements in the event of a 'no' vote in the referendum on 25 September 2005 on the extension of the agreement on free movement of persons to the new EU member states in Central and Eastern Europe. From this perspective, the 'yes' vote implies that the question of an association agreement is now moot.

The position of the various Swiss officials interviewed varied considerably on this issue. Overall, however, most Swiss officials seem sceptical of the idea of an association agreement for the purpose of coordinating the bilateral agreements. According to the majority of those interviewed, an overarching coordination (or 'chapeau') committee would not be a good instrument to improve the effectiveness and coordination of the institutional framework. The most frequent argument used against such a committee was that it would politicise the existing dialogue, which is mainly of a non-political and technical nature. Such a committee would necessarily entail more expenditure and complexity without improving the efficiency of the agreements. Another concern expressed was the fear that the amicable and cooperative spirit with which solutions are pursued in the joint committees could be lost by the establishment of a higher-level committee.

A perhaps more promising idea to improve coordination would be a more ambitious proposal to merge the various joint committees into one association committee, similar to the EEA Joint Committee and indeed most other senior officials institutions in EU external relations agreements. This would however require renegotiation of the entire set of bilateral sectoral agreements, a prospect neither side is likely to support.

The interviewees on the EU side were also mostly against the idea of an association agreement to coordinate existing agreements (the 'chapeau' idea). However, some interlocutors, both on the EU and on the Swiss side

---

[77] See "Schweiz und EU prüfen Rahmenvertrag" in *Neue Zürcher Zeitung*, 28 September 2005, p. 14.

in Brussels, argued on the contrary that such a coordination committee could be useful exactly in order to politicise issues and provide linkages between various policy areas as a means of finding acceptable overall solutions in case of multiple blockages on different dossiers.

Some Swiss interlocutors were in favour of improving coordination of the bilateral agreements by establishing an institutionalised joint committee at the ministerial level. For the interlocutors on the EU side, while agreeing on the need for a better political dialogue as indeed agreed at the first-ever bilateral EU-Swiss summit in 2004, the idea of an association agreement as a means of institutionalising this high-level political dialogue was not regarded favourably. It would in this view be better if such dialogue took place on an ad hoc basis. Another possibility would be to integrate a high-level dialogue in the 1972 agreement.

The experience concerning the political dialogue in the EEA and other association agreements between the EU and non-member states over the last decade is relevant in the debate on a possible association agreement between the EU and Switzerland. The initial idea when the EEA agreement was concluded was that the EEA Council would consist of the 15 foreign ministers of the EU, the three foreign ministers of the EEA states and the European Commissioner for External Relations. Over time, however, a practice developed whereby the EU side was represented not by the foreign ministers of the member states and then Commissioner, but by their deputies or senior officials. This model was increasingly seen as unsatisfactory, not just for the EEA but also in general for the EU's hugely expanding set of association agreements. The size of the association councils (in the case of the EEA consisting of 19 principals at the time) was found to be too cumbersome, with most of the time consumed by formal statements. In mid-2000, the EU streamlined its participation in all association councils, including the EEA. Instead of the EU-15 model, the EU is now represented by a 'Troika', consisting of the foreign minister of the rotating EU Presidency, the relevant European Commissioner and the High Representative for the CFSP. While this facilitates the proceedings and improves the possibilities for a real debate among the interlocutors, the absence of the member states reduces the potential significance of the political dialogue.

In part to respond to these changes, the idea of an upgrade or an update of the EEA agreement was briefly raised in EFTA and discussed informally between the EEA states and the Commission in 2001 and 2002.

Several possibilities were debated, from a technical update to take account of legal changes in the EU since the signing of the EEA to a more comprehensive upgrade of the agreement to incorporate other agreements such as the Schengen association, enhanced political dialogue and greater participation in decision-shaping. However, the EU's response was negative and the idea was subsequently dropped.

The regular meetings that take place between the EFTA states and the EU outside of the EEA institutions are in any case probably more important than the political dialogue conducted within the EEA framework. In the case of Norway, these include the meetings between the Norwegian Prime Minister and the EU Presidency held at the beginning of each Presidency and the annual lunch meetings between EU and EEA finance ministers. The Norwegian Foreign Minister normally also meets bilaterally with EU colleagues and EU representatives in connection with meetings of the EEA Council. The most frequent meetings between Norway and the EU at a high political level are however those that take place on an *ad hoc* basis, between EU representatives and Norwegian ministers, bilaterally with EU member state governments or multilaterally, and increasingly consultations through Norway's multiple association arrangements with the EU (CFSP, ESDP, Schengen, etc.) beyond the EEA.

In spite of these caveats, and in comparison with the less frequent and ad hoc nature of the EU-Swiss political dialogue, the institutionalised political dialogue through the EEA agreement provides a useful regular forum to discuss broader political developments. It also facilitates early participation in new EU programmes and agencies. The EFTA states in the EEA joined the EASA in mid-2005, while Swiss participation is expected only in 2006. Switzerland is experiencing similar 'queuing problems' concerning their Schengen association. The main reason why this will not be fully implemented until 2008 is that Switzerland have to wait for the full inclusion of the new EU member states into the Schengen system at the end of 2007.

An association agreement between the EU and Switzerland could provide for such an enhanced and regularised dialogue, although the experience of the EFTA states in the EEA seems to be that other irregular channels of communication and dialogue at the highest political level are perhaps more important. A regular political dialogue instituted by a possible association agreement should be regarded as a complement rather than an alternative to such ad hoc diplomacy.

6.3.2 Any role for the EEA institutions?

Switzerland already benefits from its membership in EFTA through its observer status in the EFTA Standing Committee and in the EEA Joint Parliamentary Committee, and Swiss 'social partners' participate in the EEA Consultative Committee. However, the EFTA Court and the ESA are not involved in EU-Swiss relations. One question raised in the interviews with EU and Swiss officials was whether the deficiencies encountered in the bilateral sectoral approach could be improved through use of the EFTA institutions for the EEA, the ESA and the EFTA Court.

Swiss officials were generally lukewarm to such ideas. The need for a more formal arbitration mechanism, which could be envisaged with the EFTA Court playing a role, was not seen as necessary, and the idea of giving the ESA a role in surveillance of the EU-Swiss agreements was rejected.

On the EU side, although Swiss participation in the EEA would be easier, the idea of utilising the EEA institutions did not receive any support, unless this was by way of full Swiss participation in the EEA.

6.3.3 Other proposals

Most Swiss interlocutors reacted negatively to the idea of creating a more formalised arbitration process in the joint committees than what exists in the current agreements, although some were in favour of establishing some form of mediation procedure.

A number of practical suggestions to improve the transparency of the activities of the bilateral committees emerged in the interviews. Although the nature of these committees as institutions of international law and the problem of approval by the government limit the scope of transparency, one could raise the question whether it would be possible to at least name the EU directives and regulations envisaged to be incorporated in the annexes. The interested public would then at least be in a position to inform themselves on the aims and content of those provisions.

Although Bilaterals I and II are less extensive than the EEA, they represent a significant increase in the workload of all branches of government in Switzerland. One lesson from the EEA experience is the difficulty in keeping parliament actively involved. This raises important issues for the Swiss parliament, which has relatively fewer resources available to their task of oversight of foreign affairs than do their EFTA counterparts.

Whether the system of transparency regarding the developments in the bilateral agreements should be improved with centralising measures was one of the main topics that emerged from the study. The discussion focused on the idea of establishing a 'central secretariat' either within one of the existing institutions (for instance the Federal Chancellery or the Integration Bureau) or by the creation of a new institution to improve the transparency of the activities of the joint committees.

Most interview-partners in Switzerland reacted positively to the idea of creating a centralised secretariat gathering and disseminating information from the joint committees and the involved departments. Some officials interjected that a new secretariat would be redundant, as such an institution, the Integration Bureau, already exist. More specifically, the officials in favour considered an improvement of the homepage of the Confederation's website (www.kdk.ch) to be very important. It should be updated more regularly and also linked to the departments involved with the new EU-regulation and EU jurisdiction in the specific areas. The idea was not only to inform the public in a more specific and open way about the actions in the committees, but also to provide a clear and comprehensive overview of ECJ rulings and EU *acquis* incorporated into all of the agreements, for instance through a federal website with a list of EU *acquis* in the different agreements. The European Commission is currently establishing a delegation in Berne, which could contribute to enhancing the information flow, accessibility and transparency.

Better coordination and more resources are obvious remedies to resolve or reduce the main apprehensions of Swiss officials concerning the lack of transparency and information. The EEA experience has shown the importance of political will to follow developments in the EU to take full advantage of the opportunities of decision-making provided by the agreement. It further showed, however, that the EU associated state should have no illusions as to the limits of decision-shaping and the importance the EU attaches to its own decision-making autonomy.

6.4   A new approach for EU-Swiss relations

The bilateral agreements are functioning well. There is broad support for the bilateral sectoral approach in Switzerland. In a comparative perspective, the relationship with Switzerland is closer and better than most in EU external relations, and the EU is unlikely to request any fundamental change in EU-Swiss relations in the foreseeable future. There are however several arguments in favour of an assessment of the more fundamental alternatives, as opposed to more limited improvements and adaptations, to the bilateral sectoral approach that has characterised EU-Swiss relations over the last half-century.

One reason is the prospect of further referenda in Switzerland. Popular votes on the relationship with the EU have become almost annual events in Switzerland. Uncertainty about the outcome of the referendum on the extension of the free movement of persons to the new member states in Central and Eastern Europe on 25 September 2005 raised the prospect of abrogation of many of the bilateral agreements. Had the Swiss people rejected this extension, the EU would not have been able to accept the resulting discrimination between the citizens of old and new member states, and would in all likelihood have withdrawn from the agreement. This would in turn have triggered the so-called 'guillotine clause' and the termination of an additional five agreements of Bilateral I. Moreover, the unravelling would probably not have ended there. According to the EU, an agreement on free movement of labour was a fundamental requirement for Swiss inclusion in the Schengen area, although there are no legal provisions linking the two. A termination of the agreement on free movement of persons between the EU and Switzerland would thus likely trigger an EU withdrawal from the Schengen association agreement with Switzerland. This agreement is linked legally to the Dublin association agreement on asylum, which Switzerland is now set to join. To sum up, a rejection of a protocol to one agreement in Bilateral I could all too easily have resulted in the termination of about half of the agreements of Bilaterals I and II, most of which have no direct relevance to the protocol extending the agreement on free movement of persons to the new EU member states in Central and Eastern Europe.

While the extension was supported by a comfortable majority of 56% on that occasion, future enlargements of the EU might not be as popular in Switzerland. A protocol on the extension of the agreement on the free movement of persons to Romania and Bulgaria when they accede in 2007 or 2008 is likely to be raised by the European Commission in 2006. A protocol will also be needed to accommodate the EU accession of Croatia, which, following the imprisonment of war criminal General Gotovina in late 2005, might occur by the end of the decade. This may in due course be followed sometime during the next decade by further protocols for the accession of other currently acknowledged candidates such as Turkey and Macedonia, and other potential members such as Albania and the rest of the former Yugoslav republics.

One cannot rule out that unexpected 'events' could occur that create demands from the EU for further agreements in areas that are politically sensitive in Switzerland, or from Switzerland in areas that are difficult for the EU. A recent example of this was the terrorist attacks of September 11, which had a significant impact on several of the agreements of Bilaterals I and II, notably those on air transport, the fight against fraud, Schengen/Dublin and taxation of savings, and raised difficult issues challenging Swiss policy related to banking secrecy. Another recent example was the electricity blackout in northern Italy in the summer of 2002, ostensibly in part a result of an accident in the Swiss electricity infrastructure. The EU has now requested an agreement on electricity infrastructure and market access.

A revival of the EU Constitution could have consequences for EU-Swiss relations in the long-term. It is not unimaginable that pressures to simplify the EU could extend also to its contractual relations in external relations. The EU would acquire a legal personality as a result of the Constitution, which would change the legal basis for relations with third countries. The adaptation of existing agreements to this new reality, which could be reduced to a practical technical matter, may be regarded as an opportunity to overhaul relations with third countries. The Constitution includes a clause providing for a new type of contractual arrangement with neighbouring countries.

Broader developments in the EU, such as the completion of the internal market and the 'area of freedom, security and justice' could give rise to further issues in EU-Swiss relations. Global developments, for instance the (eventual) completion of the Doha round of the WTO, are likely to spur developments between the EU and Switzerland in various areas. The latter example would particularly affect, for instance, agriculture and competition policy. Although there has been no global currency crisis for almost a decade, there were several in the previous decade, and one cannot rule this out in light of the profound financial imbalances in the global economy, although it is difficult to predict the consequences for the euro and the Swiss franc and its specific impact on EU-Swiss relations.

Some have predicted that the outcome of the current crisis in the EU following the French and Dutch rejections of the Constitutional Treaty will result in more variable geometry in the EU, with member states opting out of common policies in various areas. One result of this is that in substantial terms the difference between insiders 'opting out' and outsiders 'opting in' is further reduced. This is already the case in several areas of EU policy, notably on monetary union, in the field of justice and home affairs, where several non-member states have opted out of Schengen cooperation which includes non-member states, and in the ESDP, in which some member states do not participate but which includes a number of non-member states. More variable geometry will affect the definition of the scope of the various agreements. With more opt-outs from member states, the issue of 'relevance' of new *acquis* to areas of partial participation of EU member states is likely to become more prominent, and likely further limit the influence of non-member states in determining whether new *acquis* will be defined as falling within the scope of a given agreement or not.

One could not exclude the possibility that Switzerland will become less enamoured with the bilateral sectoral approach as it progresses further. One of the supposed benefits of the bilateral approach was that it was a more 'static' model compared with the more 'dynamic' EEA, giving greater autonomy to Swiss authorities to determine the scope and depth of cooperation and integration. But as this study has demonstrated, the relationship between Switzerland and the EU is highly dynamic. A formally 'static' agreement does not prevent a dynamic development of a relationship, if circumstances require a change and the parties agree. The 1972 agreement has for instance been updated and amended more than 15 times since it was negotiated. Indeed, the bilateral relationship with Switzerland has probably seen the most significant upgrade in EU external relations in recent years and has had a significant impact on the way in which Switzerland governs itself, as both the EU and Switzerland have ended up with more agreements with the other than what was sought in the early 1990s. Furthermore, as the discussion in the sections above has shown, it seems clear that this dynamism will continue over the course of the next decade, as new agreements are concluded and existing agreements are adapted, updated and renewed.

6.4.1 Alternatives to the bilateral sectoral approach

The bilateral sectoral approach was the third alternative of the Federal Council before the negotiations of Bilaterals I and II. Both of the two preferred options – full EU membership and participation in the EEA – remain open to Switzerland. One of the great challenges for the Swiss government will be to explain the pro's and con's of the bilateral sectoral approach, full EU membership and other theoretical alternatives in an open dialogue and in a transparent and coherent way.

The Swiss EU membership application is currently suspended, and although there is a simmering debate on whether or not it should be withdrawn, this seems to receive limited support in Switzerland, even if neutrality, initially the main argument against Swiss membership in the European Community, is no longer considered an obstacle. However, there is also little support for reviving the membership application. On the EU side, in spite of the supposed 'enlargement fatigue' after the rejection of the EU Constitution, Swiss membership is widely supported. In a 2005 poll of EU citizens, Switzerland was the most popular potential member of the EU, with 78% in favour of enlargement to Switzerland, and only 13% against. However, 'enlargement fatigue' has raised another obstacle to future EU enlargement (to Switzerland or any other country seeking membership), namely the prospect of referenda in EU countries. In March 2004, the French Constitution was changed so that any future treaties of EU accession require the consent of the French people in a referendum. Possible referenda on future EU enlargements have also been discussed in other EU member states such as the Netherlands and Austria. As long as the debate on the EU Constitution remains unresolved, and the Treaty of Nice remains the legal basis of the EU, enlargement beyond the accession of Romania and Bulgaria is impossible, unless the member states are able to agree on an institutional set-up that can accommodate more than 27 member states.

The EEA is also open to Switzerland. Although Bilaterals I and II entail a quantum leap of integration and cooperation between the EU and Switzerland, they remain significantly less extensive than EU relations with the EEA states. While the European Commission, which handles the day-to-day operations of EU-Swiss relations, might favour this for practical administrative reasons, the EU is highly unlikely to push for Switzerland joining the EEA and it has no support in Switzerland.

The idea of a customs union between the EU and Switzerland was raised in most of the interviews. Overall, the response was negative. On the EU side, the practical difficulties in managing the EU-Turkey customs union was cited as resulting in a general reluctance towards customs unions with third countries within the EU. Others noted a recent development towards a more pro-active trade policy in EFTA compared with the EU, with initiatives to conclude free trade agreements with non-EU countries before the EU has negotiated similar agreements with these countries. This is also taking pace on a bilateral basis, with the ongoing exploratory talks between Switzerland and the US on a possible free trade agreement as the most prominent example.

One could of course also envisage alternatives of less integration and cooperation between the EU and Switzerland. One of the claimed advantages of the sectoral approach according to the 1999 Integration Report was that it would allow Switzerland to exert a greater influence in determining the sectors subject to EU-Swiss cooperation. This does not seem to be borne out in practice. Indeed, the pressure on Switzerland to extend cooperation to areas of the EU's choosing has been greater than on the EFTA states of the EEA, seen in connection with Bilateral II and the agreements on taxation of savings, fraud, Schengen and the financial contribution. However, this is more an unfortunate coincidence in the timing of bilateral negotiations and legislative developments in the EU with the particular interests of Switzerland (notably relating to banking secrecy), rather than the result of a systemic difference between the EEA and the EU-Swiss bilateral sectoral approach. Furthermore, the 'guillotine clause' and other linkages between the EU-Swiss reduce the flexibility in fine-tuning the policy areas subject to formal cooperation, ostensibly one of the principal benefits of the sectoral approach. Attempts to halt, circumscribe or reduce cooperation in specific sectors could easily unravel a large number of the agreements reached between the EU and Switzerland, making a slight downgrading of cooperation and integration highly problematic.

6.5   A unique Swiss model?

To what extent can one speak of a unique 'Swiss model' of integration without EU membership? The bilateral sectoral approach pursued by Switzerland in its relationship with the EU is sometimes regarded as a unique model of how third countries could relate the Union. It is indeed the result of the national specificities of Switzerland and the particular historical context in which the principal agreements were negotiated. Some EU officials claimed that the EU would not have accepted an agreement on free movement of persons without any explicit reference to the *acquis* had Bilateral I been negotiated today. The services agreement was a first victim of the EU's new less flexible approach in terms of acknowledging the *acquis* as the explicit reference and no acceptance of permanent derogations. Indeed, the EU's flexibility has in all likelihood been further reduced after the negotiations of Bilateral II were concluded, due to the May 2004 enlargement. Switzerland is not particularly high on the agenda of the new member states.

The reduced tolerance towards exceptions and the greater difficulties in reaching any agreement within the Council make it even more arduous to agree on comprehensive packages of cooperation with third countries such as Bilaterals I and II. This reduces the scope for an *a la carte* approach to the *acquis* by third countries. Instead, the selection of topics proceeds on a *quid pro quo* basis, with concessions granted in one agreement offset by commitments in other areas. Officials interviewed for this study claimed for instance that EU support for Bilateral II, and the Schengen association and its specific derogations in particular, depended on agreement on the financial contribution.

A key feature of the Swiss model is the sectoral nature of contractual relations. This is often contrasted with the comprehensive nature of the EEA, as well as other associations such as the Europe agreements, the Stability and Association agreements with the Western Balkans, etc. This difference is however less than it may appear. First, bilateralism is the dominant approach in EU external relations, and the EEA is the main exception that confirms this rule. Secondly, most third countries with extensive ties to the EU have indeed a number of sectoral contractual arrangements beyond their principal framework agreements. Over time, these are becoming an increasingly important element of the overall relationships. This is in part a result of the pillar structure of the EU and its complex legal personality. The EU Constitution included provisions to abolish the pillar structure and give legal personality to the Union as such. As long as the constitutional crisis remains unresolved, the institutional complexity of EU external relations is likely to continue to grow.

The Swiss model stands out not so much because of the bilateral sectoral approach, but rather the absence of a comprehensive overarching bilateral 'framework' agreement. In most cases, a comprehensive bilateral agreement provides the framework for the conduct and development of relations between these third countries and the EU. Interaction takes place in a single set of institutions. The typical format consists of a cooperation/association council at the foreign ministers/commissioner level, a cooperation or association committee at the level of senior officials supported by a set of sectoral sub-committees of experts and lower-level officials. This executive branch structure is accompanied by a parliamentary committee consisting of representatives of third-country national parliaments and the European Parliament. In many cases the official institutions are supplemented by institutions and/or mechanisms of dialogue between non-state actors (trade unions, industry federations, business, etc). Although the 1972 agreements could be regarded as such a 'framework agreement', it does not include provisions for a regularised and multi-faceted political dialogue as is typically the case in such agreements between the EU and other non-member states.

The absence of such an overarching framework agreement means that there is less institutionalised political dialogue between the EU and Switzerland than between the EU and most other third countries. As a consequence, Swiss concerns are less likely to receive a hearing and be raised on the EU's agenda, unless the issue is also significant to any of the EU member states. Most of the officials interviewed, in particular on the EU side, emphasised that this dialogue played a limited role in the shaping of the overall relationship. Furthermore, it has not prevented the establishment of a parliamentary dialogue and the Swiss associations participate alongside and together with their European counterparts. Switzerland also enjoys additional benefits through its EFTA membership.

There are however several aspects of the experiences of the EU-Swiss bilateral sectoral agreements that could be relevant in considering the long-term perspectives of the European Neighbourhood Policy. The partial integration of EU-Swiss agreements provides a potential model for the ENP slogans 'everything but institutions' and a 'stake in the single market'. The experiences of the EU-Swiss partial integration agreements can perhaps provide some lessons that could be helpful in assessing the feasibility and likely challenges of the partial integration envisaged under the Stability and Association Process (SAP) and the ENP.

One such challenge concerns difficulties in delineating the specific areas of cooperation, which have emerged in several of the EU-Swiss agreements. This indicates the limits of the *a la carte* approach to European integration, insofar as the EU institutions regard the *acquis* as one single body of law and not simply as a set of individual and unrelated pieces of legislation.

Due to the significant differences between the agreements, one can in fact speak of several Swiss models of association with the EU. There is for instance an EU-Swiss 'air transport model'. Here the *acquis* is explicitly the legal basis of cooperation, and the EU institutions – the European Commission and the European Court of Justice – have competences in surveillance and arbitration in specified areas (in this case competition and state aid policies in the field of civil aviation). The Schengen association agreements provide another model differing from the standard EU cooperation and association agreements. The 'Schengen association model' goes further in granting access to the decision-making process in EU institutions than any other EU third-country agreement. Representatives of the associated states here participate with a say, but not a vote, in the EU Council of Ministers machinery (in the guise of the Schengen Mixed Committee) at the level of experts, junior and senior officials and ministers. As in the 'air transport model', participation of the associated state is explicitly based on the *acquis*.

These two agreements could provide ideas for the EU's fledgling European Neighbourhood Policy (ENP), for instance by giving the European Court of Justice a greater role in the process of providing the ENP partners a 'stake in the single market' (the 'Swiss air transport' model) or giving the neighbours a more inclusive role in the decision-shaping and processes within the EU (the 'Schengen association model').

The 1999 Integration Report predicted that the growing size of the EU constituted one of the principal challenges of the bilateral sectoral approach. This seems to have been borne out in practice. With more member states it is more difficult to reach agreement within the EU and consequently there is less flexibility in negotiating with third parties. In EU-Swiss relations, as with other EU neighbours, the 'equivalence of law' has been replaced with 'adoption of the *acquis*'. For other EU associates, it has in addition entailed also a gradual *de facto* downgrading of the political dialogue. Indeed, obtaining special privileges and specific exemptions is likely to become increasingly difficult for any third country wishing to cooperate and integrate with a deepening and enlarging EU.

This poses particular challenges for countries such as Switzerland, which seems to take special pride in its exceptionalism. Indeed, broader European and global developments over the last couple of decades have reduced the significance of many of the key elements on which Swiss identity is based. The end of the Cold War limited the need for a neutral Switzerland, both its good offices in international politics in general and the use of Switzerland as a venue for meetings between the superpowers. This occurred at a time of relative economic decline of Switzerland, which for much of the post-war period had been regarded as an island of stability and good economic governance. But as the economic governance and development in the rest of Western Europe improved, to some extent in response to further European integration, the relative attractiveness of Switzerland gradually eroded. Finally, with Bilaterals I and II, Switzerland has entered into an extensive set of contractual arrangements with the EU, as have virtually all countries in and around Europe. Indeed, with the exception of its EFTA partners in the EEA, Switzerland provides the most ambitious example of integration without EU membership today.

SOURCES AND REFERENCES

Principal sources

Official websites

The websites of the EU (europa.eu.int) and the Swiss Integration Bureau (www.europa.admin.ch.) include the texts of the agreements, other official documents and explanatory texts. Further information can be found on various websites of the Swiss government and the federal ministries and the cantons (www.admin.ch; www.kdk.ch; www.bfm.admin.ch; www.bj.admin.ch; www.ejpd.admin.ch; www.bav.admin.ch; www.europa.eu.int/eur-lex; www.aviation.admin.ch; and www.seco.admin.ch), and of the EU (europa.eu.int/comm/index_en.htm; ue.eu.int; and www.europarl.eu.int). The websites of other international organisations, notably of EFTA (www.efta.int), the WTO (www.wto.org) and the OECD (www.oecd.org) also provide relevant information.

Interviews and seminar

The authors conducted more than 20 interviews with EU and Swiss officials and experts between July and October 2005. A seminar with experts and EU and Swiss officials to discuss the preliminary conclusions of this study was organised at CEPS on 26 October 2005.

References

Arnorsson, Audunn (2004), "Ten Years with the EEA: Expectations and Experiences", in EFTA Parliamentary Committee and Consultative Committee, *The EEA and EFTA in a New Europe*, conference report, 21 October.

Balzacq, Thierry, Didier Bigo, Sergio Carrera and Elspeth Guild (2006), *Security and the Two-Level Game: The Treaty of Prüm, the EU and the Management of Threats*, CEPS Working Document No. 236, Centre for European Policy Studies, Brussels, January.

Church, Clive (2002), *Switzerland: An Overlooked Case of Europeanization?*, Queen's Papers on Europeanization No. 3, Queen's University, Belfast.

Claes, Dag Harald and Bent Sofus Tranøy (eds) (1999), *Utenfor, annerledes og suveren: Norge under EØS-avtalen (Outside, different and sovereign: Norway under the EEA agreement)*, Oslo: Arena/Fagbokforlaget.

Cottier, Thomas and Christophe Germann (2001), "Die Partizipation bei der Aushandlung neuer völkerrechtlicher Bindungen: Verfassungsrechtliche Grundlagen und Perspektiven", in Daniel Thürer, Jean-François Aubert and Jörg Paul Müller (eds), *Verfassungsrecht der Schweiz*, Zürich.

Dessemontet, F. and T. Ansay (2004), *Introduction to Swiss Law*, Third edition, Zürich.

Emerson, Michael, Marius Vahl and Steven Woolcock (2002), *Navigating By the Stars – Norway, the European Economic Area and the European Union*, CEPS paperback, Centre for European Policy Studies, Brussels.

European Commission (1993), *Future relations with Switzerland*, Communication from the Commission, COM (93) 486 final.

Fleiner, Thomas, Alexander Misic and Nicole Töpperwien (2005), *Swiss Constitutional Law*, Berne.

Goetchel, Laurent (2004), "The Swiss-EU Bilateral Agreements: A model for integration?", in EFTA Parliamentary Committee and Consultative Committee, *The EEA and EFTA in a New Europe*, conference report, 21 October.

Häfelin, Ulrich and Walter Haller (2001), Schweizerisches Bundesstaatsrecht, Fifth edition, Zürich.

Hewitt Associates (2002), *Bilateral agreement with the EU on free movement of persons (Switzerland)*, Special Edition, May.

Honegger, Edith (2004), Die gemischten Ausschüsse in den Sektoriellen Abkommen zwischen der Schweiz und der EG, Chavannes-Lausanne.

Łazowski, Adam (2005), "European Union and Switzerland: Inevitable partners?", paper presented at the NOSPA conference, 11-13 August, Reykjavik (http://registration.yourhost.is/nopsa2005/papers/Lazowski%20Switzerland%20Reykjavik%202005.doc).

Mach, Andre, Silja Hausermann and Yannis Papadopoulos (2003), "Economic regulatory reforms in Switzerland: Adjustment without European integration, or how rigidities became flexible", *Journal of European Public Policy*, 10:2, April, pp. 301-318.

Melsæther, Jan Kåre and Ulf Sverdrup (2004), *The parliamentary challenge in the EU and the EEA: An increasing gap*, ARENA Working Paper Series, No. 17, Centre for European Studies, University of Oslo.

Müller, George (2001), "Verfassungsrecht der Schweiz", in Daniel Thürer, Jean-François Aubert and Jörg Paul Müller (eds), *Rechtsetzung und Staatsverträge*, No. 38, Vol. 70, Zürich.

Nei til EU: Nei til EU's Motmelding en analyse av Norges muligheter utenfor EU og et kritisk blikk på EUs utvikling ("Counter-report of the Norwegian 'No to the EU'-movement, an analysis of Norway's possibilities outside the EU and a critical view of the development of the EU"), Oslo, 2001.

Patten, Chris (2005), *Not Quite the Diplomat – Home Truths About World Affairs*, London: Penguin/Allan Lane.

Ramsauer, Rudolf (2005), "2005: une année cruciale dans les relations économiques entre la Suisse et l'Union européenne", speech, Brussels, 12 October.

Riksrevisjonen (2005), *Riksrevisjonens undersøkelse av forvaltningens arbeid med utformingen av EØS-relevant regelverk* (The Auditor General's analysis of the work of the administration in the development of EEA-relevant rules and regulations), Riksrevisjonens Administrative Report No. 2.

Ruspekhofer, Silvia (2005), "Schengen/Dublin und darüber hinaus: An den Grenzen des eidgenössischen Bilateralismus – Völker- und Europarecht AKTUELL", *Jusletter*, 18 July.

Sverdrup, Ulf and Stephan Kux (1997), *Balancing Effectiveness and Legitimacy in European Integration – The Norwegian and the Swiss Case*, ARENA Working Paper Series, No. 31, Centre for European Studies, University of Oslo.

Swiss Government (1999), Integration Report, Bern.

Thürer, Daniel, Rolf H. Weber and Roger Zäch (eds) (2002), *Bilaterale Verträge Schweiz – EG, Ein Handbuch*, Zürich.

Vahl, Marius (2004), "Whither the Common European Economic Space? Political and Institutional Aspects of Closer Economic Integration between the EU and Russia," in Tanguy de Wilde d'Estmael and Laetitia Spetschinsky (eds), *La politique étrangerè de la Russie et l'Europe*, P.I.E. Lang, pp. 167-199.

STATISTICAL ANNEX

Basic figures (2004)

	European Union	Switzerland
Population	457 million	7.3 million
GDP	€12,691 billion	€288 billion
GDP/capita	€27,770	€39,637

Source: Switzerland: European Commission, DG Trade. EU: Eurostat, World Bank.

Economic growth, 1996-2004

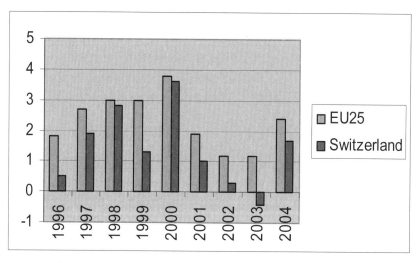

Source: IMF World Economic Outlook, September 2005. Own calculations for EU 25 average.

The EU's 10 major trading partners (2004)

Partners		Trade volume (€ billion)	%
World		1,993	100.0
1	US	391	19.7
2	China	175	8.8
3	Switzerland	136	6.8
4	Russia	126	6.3
5	Japan	116	5.9
6	Norway	86	4.4
7	Turkey	68	3.5
8	Korea	48	2.4
9	Canada	38	1.9
10	Taiwan	36	1.8

Source: European Commission, DG Trade.

Switzerland's 10 major trade partners (2004)

Partners		Trade volume (€ billion)	%
World		199	100.0
1	EU	138	69.5
2	US	16	8.4
3	Japan	5.4	2.7
4	China	3.8	1.9
5	Hong Kong	3.6	1.8
6	Russia	3.5	1.8
7	Turkey	2.8	1.4
8	Israel	2.6	1.3
9	Singapore	2.2	1.1
10	Canada	1.4	0.7

Source: European Commission, DG Trade.

Switzerland's trade in goods

		2000	2002	2004
Exports to the EU	Volume (€ billion)	62.3	61.4	61.5
	Share of total (%)	62.0	62.3	60.7
	Share of total EU imports (%)	6.2	6.5	5.9
Imports from the EU	Volume (€ billion)	72.4	72.6	75.0
	Share of total (%)	76.6	80.3	77.3
	Share of total EU exports (%)	8.4	8.0	7.7

Source: European Commission, DG Trade.

Switzerland's trade in services

	2001	2002	2003
Exports of services to the EU (€ billion)	31.7	32.8	31.3
Imports of services from the EU (€ billion)	39.5	38.6	41.4

Source: European Commission, DG Trade.

Switzerland's foreign direct investment

	2001	2002	2003
Swiss FDI outflows to the EU (€ billion)	7.4	7.6	18.6
EU FDI inflows to Switzerland (€ billion)	7.6	27.5	10.7

Source: European Commission, DG Trade.

LIST OF ABBREVIATIONS

APM	Agreement on Procurement Markets (WTO)
AS	Official Register of Federal Law (Amtliche Sammlung des Bundesrechts)
BAZL	Federal Civil Aviation Depertment
BBl	Bundesblatt
CHF	Swiss franc
COREPER	Committee of Permanent Representatives
CRAFT	Cooperative Research Action for Technology
DG	Directorate General (of the European Commission)
EASA	European Air Safety Agency
EC	European Community
ECJ	European Court of Justice
Ecosoc	Economic and Social Committee (of the EU)
ECSC	European Coal and Steel Community
EEA	European Economic Agreement/Area
EEA	European Environmental Agency
EEC	European Economic Community
EFTA	European Free Trade Association
EIONET	European Environment Information and Observation Network
ENP	European Neighbourhood Policy
ESA	EFTA Surveillance Authority
ESDP	European Security and Defence Policy
Europol	European Police Office

Eurostat	Statistical Office of the European Community
FP6/ FP7	EU Framework Programmes for Research and Development
GATT	General Agreement on Tariffs and Preferences
GSP	General System of Preferences
HGV	Heavy Goods Vehicle
IB	Integration Bureau/Integration Office
JPC	Joint Parliamentary Committee (of the EEA agreement)
KdK	Conference of the Cantonal Governments (Konferenz der Kantonsregierugnen)
LFG	Swiss Statute of Air Transport
NEAT	New Transalpine Railways
OEEC	Organisation for European Economic Cooperation
OECD	Organisation for Economic Cooperation and Development
PCA	Parliamentary Control of the Administration
PublG	Federal Publication Statute (Publikationsgesetz)
PublV	Federal Publication Ordinance, (Publikationsverordnung)
RTD	Research and Technical Development
R&D	Research and Development
RVOG	Federal Statute on the Organisation of the Government and Administration (Regierungs- und Verwaltungsorganistationsgesetz)
SECO	State Secretariat of Economic Affairs (Staatssekretariat für Wirtschaft)
SIS	Schengen Information System
SR	Systematic Register of Federal Law (Systematische Sammlung des Bundesrechts)
UN	United Nations
WTO	World Trade Organisation